DOLL PLAY OF
PILAGÁ INDIAN CHILDREN

DOLL PLAY *of* PILAGÁ INDIAN CHILDREN

AN EXPERIMENTAL AND FIELD ANALYSIS OF THE BEHAVIOR OF THE PILAGÁ INDIAN CHILDREN

By

JULES and ZUNIA HENRY

With a New Introduction by
STANLEY DIAMOND

VINTAGE BOOKS
A DIVISION OF RANDOM HOUSE · NEW YORK

FIRST VINTAGE BOOKS EDITION, April 1974

Library of Congress Cataloging in Publication Data (Revised)

Henry, Jules, 1904–1969.
    Doll play of Pilaga Indian children.

    Reprint of the 1944 ed. published by American Orthopsychiatric
Association, New York, which was issued as Research monographs
no. 4, American Orthopsychiatric Association.
    Bibliography: p.
    1. Pilaga Indians—Children. 2. Pilaga Indians—Psychology.
3. Indians of South America—Children. 4. Indians of South
America—Psychology. I. Henry, Zunia, joint author. II. Ti-
tle. III. Series: American Orthopsychiatric Association. Research monographs, no. 4.
F2823.P5H4 1974   301.41′7   73-19998
ISBN 0-394-71073-8

Manufactured in the United States of America

TO
RUTH BENEDICT

ACKNOWLEDGMENTS

THE field work that serves as a basis for this monograph was made possible through a grant by the Columbia University Council for Research in the Social Sciences, and much of the subsequent preparation of the manuscript was done under its auspices.

Doctors Ruth Benedict and Margaret Mead were kind enough to read the manuscript, and their suggestions as to its improvement have been very valuable.

We wish to thank the Editor of the American Journal of Orthopsychiatry for his interest in this monograph and for permission to reprint in it certain sections that appeared as original articles in that Journal.

We are especially and deeply indebted to Dr. David M. Levy who was quick to see the value of our work and gave us constant encouragement.

We are also grateful to the Buell Quain Fund for help in making the publication of this book possible.

J. AND Z. H.

February, 1943

INTRODUCTION TO THE VINTAGE EDITION

I F anthropologists have not focused clearly on women, they have turned away from children even more completely. The reasons should be obvious. The academic discipline has been dominated by male attitudes, interests, and purposes, as defined in our own society; and anthropologists who happened to be female routinely adopted these perspectives for the health of their careers. Alternatively, a few of the latter used their gender manipulatively, conducting ethnological experiments on the behavior of women (and children) with overly elegant results. In such cases, the people studied do not speak for themselves. They merely animate the presuppositions of the ethnologist, while efficiently advancing her professional status. Most anthropologists—there are, of course, sensitive and honorable exceptions—organized their material patrilaterally, that is, from the standpoint of the Western middle-class, middle-aged male ego. This is still largely the case, not only with reference to the angle of entry into and handling of subject matter—politics, social structure, material culture, ritual—but, more strikingly, with reference to method. The careerism of professional anthropologists is bound to make their methods abstract. Even, perhaps I should say *above all*, participant observation can be easily faked, becoming an ego- and ethno-centric experiment, a mere imitation of the life of the other. The purpose is then no more than to establish one's credentials or, even less creditably, to ease one's conscience at being an uninvited guest who may at any moment overstay his leave. The anthropologist, no matter how dedicated, can never resolve the contradictions of field work completely. He or she remains a stranger, if not an interloper; he cannot share the fate of those he "studies," and therefore ends up by objectifying them for the sake of his "work." This was brought home to me rather strongly some years ago while I was working on a North American Indian reservation. One of the elders spoke bitterly about a senior colleague of mine, an "expert" in that people's language and culture. "We have given him everything," this elder explained, "the language, the rituals, our lives, and he has used them. He is very big now, written many books, made much money; he would have been nothing without us. But what does he give in return? He does not help us fight our battles. He is a thief. He is not one of us. We want nothing further to do with him. He has no real understanding of us."

Actually, the anthropologist in question was rather modest and certainly not rich. But from the Indian's point of view he was an opportunist, although he had his own standard of *professional* integrity. The Indians refused to grant him the disciplinary privilege of splitting himself into a person on the one hand, a professional on the other. For them, that meant no more than a license to talk out of both sides of his mouth. Existentially, the Indians were right.

Nonetheless, there are degrees of methodological abstraction. There may also be an ultimately justifying purpose for the anthropological enterprise, namely the critique of Western civilization; but first a word about the methods. At the far end of the scale is impersonal, hard-nosed, professional, even ideological opportunism—the native is part of an experiment. At the nearer, human end is the dialectical, if impermanent, exchange of consciousness, an encounter. This means giving oneself over to the intimate life of a people, the domestic culture, within the limits of spiritual propriety, not by right, but by invitation. I will not linger on the problems and possibilities of getting to know the women and what the women know. Students more competent than I am are working at that. But children everywhere occupy unknown territory. Even in the more or less collectivized Israeli kibbutz—the object, by now, of so many formal studies of what is called "the rearing process" or "socialization"—children have their own songs, attitudes, social antennae, spontaneous play groups; that is, they have something that resembles their own culture, which both reflects the culture at large, and as in the kibbutz, may simultaneously be an effort to oppose it, an antithetical culture writ small.

Unfortunately, the pursuit of the dynamics of childhood has tended to be the prerogative of psychology or medicine, usually undertaken in the shadow of professional presuppositions. The context was, and remains, typically experimental, but if not experimental, it is hypothetical and dogmatically psychohistorical—the child is conceived as having been the inevitable father of the man. In the *experimental* case, questions are asked relevant to a problem phrased by the investigator; the conclusions obey his cultural logic. In the psychohistorical case, the child is understood as an even more profoundly determined mechanism; the cultural, symbolic play of children, their exploration of possibilities—sometimes against great odds—is neglected. Admittedly, such cultural exploration, or play, in childhood takes its cue from the restrictions and impositions of the society at large. It reveals them while elaborating on, or denying, them. It informs us not only about reality, but of realities missed. And the form and impulse of childhood play lead us beyond the frustrations and possibilities of a particular culture—revealing, perhaps, something of the atavistic dynamics of culture, generically defined. But that is a dark and dangerous subject which I have no right to impose upon this introduction.

Getting to know children—"studying them," as we say professionally—is, then, very difficult, full of surprise and paradox. Children are always learning and using what they learn as leverage to learn more within or outside of the adult world. Perhaps in a civilization such as ours, where there is a radical discontinuity between children and adults, what they learn is beyond the adult memory, and therefore beyond adult imagination. Of course, one can never get to know another human being completely; complete knowledge implies total control, and one would have to be capable of conceiving the other person as completely determined, as in some ultimate experiment. Such demonic expectations are never fulfilled.

The work of Jules and Zunia Henry, begun more than a generation ago, strains against the limits of the discipline and breaks through to emerge as a minor classic. But it is a classic between the lines; the richest themes were to be taken up more fully in Jules Henry's maturity, most notably in *Culture Against Man* and *Pathways to Madness*. In retrospect, *Doll Play of Pilagá Indian Children* is the radical beginning and must certainly have been an important source of that courageous critique of his own society that Henry was to achieve. As anthropologists know, one never forgets the kind of experience the Henrys portray. Its meanings deepen and ramify as the years go by.

It took time, effort, and a sustained freedom of spirit for them to issue, finally, not in opportunistic publication, or rationalizations for what one or one's society has become, but in the unequivocal understanding of contemporary cultural failure. There can hardly be any question that Henry's later reflections on the state of modern Western civilization—most pertinently, on the degradation of language, the socioeconomic context of psychopathology, the failure of mass education, his concern (rage is a better word) about the spiritually and/or economically impoverished lives that millions of American children are forced to live—are significantly rooted in this early field experience, an experience he shared with his wife.

One finds that the Henrys' observations are simultaneously an interpretation of Pilagá behavior and an implied or explicit critique of our own. In every important instance, the contrast is favorable to the Pilagá. We are told, for example, that "the daily experience of Pilagá children is not remorse or loss of self esteem . . . Self-punishment and self-accusation do not occur in any of the Pilagá material . . . The whole complicated apparatus of guilt—what ethnologists would call the institutional support for guilt—extending from church to sports in our culture is missing among the Pilagá. They have no penitent speeches and no confessional. Self-flagellation does not occur and they are strangers to 'gentleman's codes of honor.'" And further: "The atmosphere of sanctity, impeccability, and compulsory love with which parents in our culture surround themselves is missing among the Pilagá. Pilagá parents are much more the equals of their children. They do not demand absolute love, honor, and respect as do parents in our culture, nor do they drill into their children the 'Oh, how much I have suffered for you' theme. If a Pilagá child hesitates to insult his erring parent, it is not for fear of disturbing some cloud-enveloped holiness, but rather to avoid a blow or a dousing with cold water."

"All of these contrasting attitudes should be borne in mind," say the Henrys, "when considering the Pilagá materials." In other words, the Pilagá are not Western-civilized Christians but the primitive converse. Accordingly, "Tapáñi [a nine-year-old child] is openly called 'bad'; she is 'stingy,' she is 'ugly'; she is 'undersized'; she is an 'old lady.' With the exception of the last, poor Tapáñi is all of these. *As a matter of fact, Tapáñi would be treated much worse in our culture than she is among the Pilagá.* She is a bully and a glutton and uses her bullying to satisfy her gluttony."

We are informed that certain activities directed against the self represent the "actualization of a generalized anxiety." "The commonest is that in which a child impersonates a jaguar or a lunatic and chases all the other children with an iron wheel which he pushes before him on the end of a stick. This game is also characterized by great excitement and laughter. The children are careful not to hurt one another. . . . the thrill lies in the escape from the threat. . . . for a few moments, but repeatedly during the play, the fleeing child becomes the center of attention of the other children—and even of the dog."

It deserves note that the latter instance is offered by the Henrys as an everyday analogue of certain experimental vectors. This two-way traffic between experimental observation and cultural reality ventilates their method and is the only possible confirmation of a psycho-*logic*. They contrast their own experimental procedure with that of psychiatrist David Levy, whose study of sibling rivalry, based on projective doll play, they have ostensibly followed. It turns out that *their* dolls "represented the child's entire family," whereas Levy's always represented the same trio—mother, baby, sibling. Moreover, their dolls were named for the child's family, while Levy's dolls were simply "mother," "baby," and "brother" or "sister." Moreover, "Levy presented his children with a dramatic situation and a problem to solve ['What does she (or he) do?'],

[but] neither of these things were done in our experiments." Finally, "Levy's dolls had no genitals, ours did." They conclude that the Pilagá children, unlike those in New York, thus had the chance to act out their own scenarios—sexually, with reference to the expression of hostility, "in accordance with their own inner needs," and to do so with greater specificity and freedom. "This permitted a more complete analysis of behaviour patterns than might otherwise have been obtained."

One should add that the Henrys interacted fully with the children in an open field situation. There was no looking down from a great height, no tautological laboratory milieu, no doctor-patient relationship. Indeed, I find this ethnological sensitivity the most impressive part of their carefully documented (a fifty-page concluding section of protocols) field-experimental method. They became part of the children's world, responded to the children's moods, and learned to combine patience with spontaneity, which one must do if one is to get to know children. And when they were finished, they had in fact exploded the notion that the Western syndrome "sibling rivalry," with its resulting effects of feeling, is a cultural universal, although they themselves, working modestly, even discreetly, and still new to their vocation, made no such outright claim. What they revealed, in no uncertain terms, was that among the Pilagá, there was no guilt as we would define it, no chronic corrosion of self-esteem, no compulsive efforts at restitution for a hostility that looms larger in the imagination than in the act, and in contrast with Dr. Levy's material, little or no evidence of destruction of property, or effort to deface the image of the other.

The Henrys also established that sibling tension is *symmetrical*, a two-way street among the Pilagá—if the older resents the younger, the younger resents the older. But the parents do not consider *that* a problem; for reasons that should already be evident, the culture confronts and modulates rather than reinforces such tension.*

Gratification in infancy is luxurious: "Among the Pilagá, the entire naked body of the infant is pressed against its mother's naked body. While it sucks at one breast it manipulates the other with one hand. The Pilagá child is nursed many times a day. When the child is being carried on a sling against its mother's body the child treats the breast almost like an 'all day sucker.' "

Hence, in Pilagá doll play, there are no attacks on the breasts. In draw-

---

* Moreover, there are socially structured occasions for the expression of the hostility that is engendered in the Pilagá milieu (see p. 55), and there is a "generalized erotic attitude toward the environment."

ing the inevitable contrast, the Henrys combine a deliberate naïveté with irony: "One wonders why, since weaning is so early in our culture, and bottle feeding so common, Levy's experiments show so many attacks on the breasts." In fact, by the time they are done with their qualifications, nothing is left of the orthodox notion of sibling rivalry, except the hostile behavior of a child against his sibling. In their conclusion, they observe, tongue in cheek, "The problem naturally arises as to how far sibling rivalry is culturally determined."

They mention a number of possible cultural variations, other than those they observed among the Pilagá, which would further diminish the definition of the syndrome. "Some day," the Henrys say, "ethnologists may be able to study these problems in the field." *Some day*, when they themselves have already done the greater part of the job. I labor this point in order to help rescue this admirable work from what has been the prevailing psychiatric misunderstanding—namely, that it *substantiates* our concept of sibling rivalry. One medical reviewer even claimed that the Henrys had tried to put sibling rivalry on a purely biological basis. I do not bring this matter to the reader's attention in order to score points against psychiatric colleagues; the issue is more serious and complex than that. What is at stake is the use and meaning of language. Ethnologists who follow their experiences with fidelity, as do the Henrys, are in a position to realize the inadequacy of Western categorical schemes, "scientific" or otherwise, with reference to other, particularly primitive cultures. Conversely, scientists or scholars in our society are convinced that their classifications are universally valid; with minor adjustments they can subsume the whole of human experience. It is fair to note, however, that this ethnocentric illusion is not dispelled by the strategy of presentation of much ethnological material, which tends to be orthodox, within the standard Western conceptual scheme; the ethnologist is, after all, trained in the Western academy. Against that latter inevitability, irony, although not a preventative, is a useful antidote, and the Henrys use it well.

But most of the time, in drawing the contrast with their own cultural milieu, they are direct: Pilagá children do not suck their thumbs, and the "kind of . . . narcotic-like finger-sucking that worries parents and physicians in our culture does not occur among the Pilagá at all." Nor are they "temper-tantrum" children, although temper tantrums do occur. They do not stammer, suffer night terrors, vomit unless seriously ill, or mimic their elder siblings. They can, I think, be described as autonomous, within the limits of their necessary dependence on adults, and the adults' necessary dependence on *their* means for reproducing life in their society. It follows that "Pilagá children are never negativistic or destructive." This is certainly related to the fact that the "commonest symptoms of maladjustment" go unpunished, "hence the problems do not become intensified."

"Thus"—and if I were to choose a fitting conclusion to this pioneering work it would be in this sentence—"most of the behaviour traits which, in our society, lead a thoughtful parent to consider a child in need of psychiatric care, either do not occur or are ignored among the Pilagá." I find that, along with other observations including those already noted, fully in accord with my own ethnological experience. More to the point, it foreshadows what was to become a lifelong preoccupation for Jules Henry.

The monograph has long since outgrown the psychiatric and relativistic auspices under which it was launched.

FOREWORD

Iᴛ is fortunate that Dr. and Mrs. Jules Henry's detailed studies of the play of the Pilagá Indian children are now in print. In spite of many diverse circumstances, they have succeeded in fortifying observations of the rivalries and jealousies of children in a remote primitive tribe with a standardized setting. In spite of the difficulties in following the play of numerous children, under constant distraction, they have succeeded by carefully recording and analyzing numerous protocols, in extracting the individual experience. In that way it becomes possible to follow the play of sibling rivalry for each subject, and accumulate data for comparative studies.

The Henrys were able, furthermore, to achieve that orientation so necessary in this type of investigation—a kind of cultural identification. In other words, they lived the life of the tribe, became fully conversant with their language and customs, and keenly aware, through first hand experience, of the family relationships. The sibling rivalry studies represent only one of a number of studies in this volume. Other topics are concerned with the various facets of family life, cultural determinants of behavior, besides interesting interpretations of the psychodynamics involved. A special point is made of sibling rivalry experiments in this foreword. It is worth repeating that this is only one of a number of studies described in this book.

The sibling rivalry experiment, depicting through play with dolls an older child observing the nursing baby at the mother's breast, is as real a situation in the lives of primitive children as in the lives of our own children.* It gives us a ready gauge of the expression of feelings of jealousy and hostility, making possible generalizations about responses of a child to a basic problem in family adjustment. This comparative method enables us to determine how far the behavior is basic to the family situation as such, and how it varies according to cultural determinants. To use the word "biological" in a rather loose sense, it enables us to differentiate between reactions biologically and culturally determined. Regardless of the diversity of family organization, the sibling rivalry situation is encountered in both patriarchal and matriarchal groups. It represents a universal experience whenever a mother has more than one child in her own

* For the purpose of this foreword, I have utilized excerpts from my article, *Sibling Rivalry in Children of Primitive Groups*, which appeared in the American Journal of Orthopsychiatry, IX, 1, p. 205, 1939. (S-R=sibling rivalry.)

care. It is part and parcel, therefore, of the biology of maternal function. The word "sociobiological" or "psychobiological" might be preferable in this connection, but the meaning implied is clear, namely, that we are dealing, for all practical purposes, with a universal situation among people regardless of their various cultural forms, arising directly out of biologic behavior.

In the Henry experiments, children were not isolated with the examiner because of external circumstances. One or more children were present. Dolls were used and given names to represent the child's own family. To make sure of the identification, the child was asked to repeat the names given. After the dolls were presented and the names used, the child was given clay. In the first experiments some of the children tried to put genitalia on the dolls to differentiate the sex. Later on the examiner made the genital difference part of the experiment. If breasts were not made and placed on the mother, this was suggested. If the baby was not placed on the breast, this was suggested. From that point on, there was very little activity on the part of the examiner. The introductory phrases of the standard sibling rivalry experiments were not used.

Since in most cases several children were in the room, it was difficult to keep only one child at play with the material selected. The examiner used toys to distract the other children and to keep them away from the play material depicting the family. This was not always possible, so that various complications in the play situation arose. Child A, for example, would play with the dolls representing his family, manipulating them in various ways and talking about them, whereupon Child B would enter and utilize the same material; Child C might do likewise. The protocols record in any one session the activities of several children going on simultaneously or in succession. Since various combinations of children were used repeatedly, the observer, in going over the protocols, would extract all the material pertaining to the particular subject. In that way the situations described represent free play activity of children with dolls, usually representing the members of their own family, in which the activity of the examiner might consist in emphasizing the fact by words or by manipulation of objects that the baby was at the mother's breast.

The use of clay genitalia on every doll is another complicating factor. The protocols show a remarkable amount of sexual data. This is explained by the observers as a peculiar cultural phenomenon of this group. In how far this phase of the culture was given special emphasis by the use of clay genitalia might be clarified by using situations in which such methods were not employed, in which each child was observed alone. This, of course, would have been impossible in the group studied, since the structure of the hut and the activities of the children in their small and highly compact village made it impossible to conduct the experiment along other lines. In the main, it is possible to trace through, in the methods used, the varying utilizations of the material by each child. The essential dynamics of the play are the same as in the sibling rivalry experiments performed in New York City. In most instances, the play of hostility does not mount, as in the S-R experiments. They would keep well within the classification of mild to moderate display of hostility, chiefly mild. There is a greater use of insulting epithets in contrast with the display of hostility by actual damage to the objects, illustrated in the New York group. This may mean a greater inhibition of hostile movements or, of course, it may be due to the fact that the S-R experiments were designed to aid in the mounting of hostility, especially by the use of words for the purpose of eliciting hostility—a device that was not employed with the Pilagás.

Several excerpts from the play of one of the children in the group will illustrate these difficulties. A four year old boy, who had a younger brother aged one year and an older sister aged nine, reacted to the mother doll by putting his face close to her breast and making sucking movements. The next day, in his play with the dolls, he placed the sister doll and the one which had been given his own name at the breast. On the third occasion, he shook his fist at the sister doll and said, "Stop it." This he repeated and then made sucking noises over the mother doll's head. He then shook his fist at the mother doll. This was followed by putting the doll representing himself between the legs of the mother doll, saying, "They are having intercourse." During a fourth period with the play material he placed the doll representing himself on top of the sister doll, then played that a toy turtle was biting the "self doll" many times. Then he had the turtle bite the mother doll, then the sister doll, saying, "It bites my sister." He then put away the sister, mother and brother dolls, saying, "They are far away." He then had the turtle bite the doll representing himself. On another occasion he put the doll representing his baby brother under the mother doll and said, "Intercourse." Then he put the sister doll and the doll representing himself on the mother doll's back, picked up a knife, placed it over the sister doll's throat and said, "I killed her." He cut off her vagina and said, "I kill her vagina." He then cut out her vagina, then the belly, and then cut the throat of the doll representing himself, and finally the penis, saying, "I cut off my penis." He then put the brother doll over the mother doll, penis to vagina and mouth to breast, mentioning the brother's name. Then he put the doll representing himself next to the sister doll, put aside the mother and brother doll, finally restoring the brother doll to the breast of the mother doll, saying, "I'll stop."

This will do as a typical illustration. The jealousy and hostility toward the baby, the resulting self-punishment, and the final restoration of the baby to the mother's breast, are clearly revealed. "I'll stop," now seems to indicate that, with the restoring act, the dramatic play is completed. The immediate regression to the nursing position initiates a series of play activities. His attempt to push the others away in order to get back on the breast seems clear. The jealousy and hostility veer toward the younger brother and older sister. The use of castration as a self-punishment device seems equated with the hostile attack on the sister's vagina. That the baby at the breast carries also the meaning of sexual relations, another source of jealousy, might be inferred. However, the fact that organs of the sexes are depicted in clay would act in itself as a stimulus for their connection. The records reveal many instances in which each male doll is made to copulate with each female doll. The influence of the play material as a primary determinant of the play dynamics can be understood by a logical analysis of all the data. There is, also, unusual freedom of sexual activity among the children and adults of this tribe. There is frequent play of hostility against the father because of his sexual intimacy with the mother, and easy utilization of sexual intercourse between dolls representing mothers and children. The cultural determinants of these activities are fully analyzed by the Henrys in this publication.

DAVID M. LEVY, M.D.

TABLE OF CONTENTS

I. INTRODUCTION

THIS monograph is a report of the results of doll experiments conducted by us among Pilagá Indian children. It is by no means a complete statement of the results of our studies. It is purposely limited to an analysis of the responses of Pilagá children to an experimental situation. Further material on Pilagá child life will appear in a later publication. Our purpose here is to provide psychologists, psychiatrists, and anthropologists with a reference for a comparative study of certain types of problems, and to present a demonstration of a technique in anthropological field method.

Since David Levy's classic work on sibling rivalry[1] has served in great part as a theoretical orientation for our work, since he has sharply focused certain types of problem, and because he has developed a very precise technique for presenting the material, we have followed him closely in many respects. This, we believe, has the advantage of making quick comparisons possible. The reader will note, however, that our results are often quite different from his. This is natural in a strange culture, and it would be surprising indeed if our results were the same. Certain differences between Levy's results and ours are due also to differences in procedure.

The purpose of our experiments was, first of all, to see what could be obtained in a primitive culture through the use of a projective technique developed in our own culture. When we saw, however, that the procedure focused sharply many of the problems on which we were collecting field notes, we decided to use it as a definite field tool as much as possible.

In the employment in a strange culture of an experimental procedure developed in our own, problems of interpretation necessarily arise. How shall an act performed by a child in an experiment be interpreted? Does the act performed in the experiment really show what it seems to show? The only way to solve these problems is to *check the experimental results with direct field observation*, and we have tried throughout our work to document every experimental act with observations from the actual life of the children. It can be seen that such a procedure gives a special validity to the experimental results, and that the experimental results give a special validity to the field observation. We have not always been

---

[1] *Sibling Rivalry*. Research Monograph Series, No. 2. American Orthopsychiatric Association, 1937.

successful, however, in our attempt to find real-life parallels to experimental evidence, and the reader will find that in a number of cases, therefore, we have drawn none or very tentative conclusions.

Unlike the psychiatrist in our own culture whose first-hand knowledge of his patients is generally limited to the consultation hour, and who must supplement this with reports of parents or social workers, our material was always before us. The children were always about—playing in our house, climbing on our laps, and eternally watching us—and the adults were constant visitors. For our part, we spent a great deal of time in the children's homes conversing and observing. Thus we had many opportunities to see at first hand what the psychiatrist is frequently forced to infer. Observation itself, however, is a technical procedure. One must know *what* to look for and *how* to look for it. One must have learned from Freud and Melanie Klein that the minute details of life and movement are charged with significance, and one must have learned from David Levy that movements follow each other in meaningful related sequences. One must have absorbed fully the deep import of Margaret Mead's essay on *More Comprehensive Field Methods*[2] so that one will realize that events are important even if they are not dressed up in feathers and ushered in by the beating of drums and the blare of trumpets. The minute, unformalized detail of life is of enormous significance for the study of child development. Indeed, our own study often falls short just where we failed to record enough of these minute details.

How to observe these details, however, is another problem. It seems to us that the primary rule should be to keep one's eyes fixed on the situation. Village life is full of distractions, but a situation left in the middle is a situation lost. It may never repeat itself during the field trip. So it has been our practice to watch any play of events—whether it be a mother nursing her child or children tumbling about—until the situation has changed. The problem naturally arises as to how to record—not everyone can watch and write at the same time.[3] We followed three procedures. At times we wrote while the situation was unfolding. At other times we watched the situation until it changed into a different one and then immediately wrote it down as fully as possible. Still other events were dictated by one of us while the other wrote.

For the ethnologist who cannot write without looking at the page, the technique of watching until the situation changes has the advantage that the ethnologist sees the whole thing and records the basic structure of the

[2] American Anthropologist 35, No. 1. January–March 1933.
[3] A possible solution is the use of the stenotype.

situation even though he may omit some details. If he trains himself he can reduce the number of details he distorts or forgets. It must be stressed, however, that the recording must be done *immediately* after the situation has changed, for memory loss and distortion are constant processes. For the ethnologist who must look at the page while he writes, the disadvantages of recording *during the action*, however, seem still greater, for he must necessarily lose a great deal while he is looking at his notebook. The best technique is, perhaps, to have one person write while another describes events as they take place before him. When there are only two ethnologists this is often not possible, for each has his own part of the field work to cover. A possible solution is to employ natives who can write while the ethnologist dictates. This we were unable to do, for the problem of teaching illiterate persons to write rapidly enough to be useful in this capacity was too great, and the time was too short.

Once the Pilagá realized that we were their well-wishers—that we were their friends in all situations, would always help them in time of need, and were general economic assets—they put up with a great deal. The ethnologist who fixes his eyes on a woman while she is nursing a baby or making a pot will be more easily tolerated if he is socially useful, undemanding, and emotionally controlled. It is true that at times our gazing somewhat embarrassed the Pilagá and distorted situations a little, but it must always be borne in mind that unless the ethnologist tells him, the native does not know that his unconscious attitudes are the subject of study. Hence the distortion will often be in a direction that does not fundamentally alter the situation. Indeed, the native's very embarrassment may throw into relief processes otherwise hidden—as, for example, in the case of the mother who, embarrassed by steady observation of her and her infant son, suddenly picked up the child and, in an obviously over-demonstrative burst of sentiment, kissed him resoundingly on the penis. If an embarrassed mother nurses her child *too* often, or bounces him *too* vigorously on her lap, or coos *too* sentimentally, it is of profound importance to the investigator.

It must not be imagined that we wandered about the village silent and staring. On the contrary, we conversed and at times were even garrulous. Often, therefore, observation went on during conversation. Sometimes, however, conversation just died, and so observation became reduced to simple watching. The impression this watching seemed to create was that we were fond of the baby. Sometimes while we were watching a situation in one part of the house a Pilagá in another part would try persistently to engage us in conversation. This naturally would tend to make precise observation of the particular situation difficult. The feeling that we were their friends, however, was quite sufficient to get us over this difficulty as well as over many others, and under these circumstances the Pilagá were quite able to accept our uninterested, laconic answers with equanimity, especially since they frequently answer this way themselves.

The sensitive ethnologist may feel loath to "treat his subjects like guinea pigs," but it is difficult to see how the kind of delicate and precise observation needed for child study can be carried out without a certain callousness in this regard. The study of an infant in any situation calls for the same kind of intense concentration as the observation of a slide under a microscope. Where one of the investigators can use a ciné camera the strain of observation is somewhat reduced; but even here, it seems to us, the person who is not photographing still has just as difficult a time writing in the social context while his companion photographs.

The older Pilagá children were quite easy to observe. On the other hand, attention intoxicated them and their activities were apt to become too intense if an adult watched. Once, for example, Tapáñi began to lay down and pick up her baby brother over and over again as soon as she observed that while her baby brother was throwing himself about in a tantrum, both of them were being photographed. She was delighted at the attention she received. Nor shall we forget soon the rolling, tumbling, gyrating show three year old Mátakana put on when she got the attention of one of us for twenty-five uninterrupted minutes. Hence, often the observation of the children had to be carried out with circumspection so that the games would not be stepped up to an unusual pitch of intensity. This was the principal problem in the observation of the children over two years of age. They were always eager to have us around and at times even informed us in advance of their activities. Conversation with them was easy. On the whole, Pilagá children are more outspoken than adults, although they have much the same blocks when unconscious processes or areas of the culture which are emotionally highly charged are in question.

Distributions of candy, sugar, and *yerba mate*[4] were obvious procedures to win the children; but we also fed crowds of them during the hungry time. Equally important, however, was a frankly receptive attitude and the absence of aggressive behavior on our part, except where special situations made it absolutely necessary. Since we had no "pet" child, we did not alienate the other children through undue attention to one of their number. The fact that we lived in a separate house, and were not bound by

[4] Paraguayan tea.

strong kinship ties to anyone were important factors in making our house a kind of hangout. Although our hut was only about 10′×13′ and full of cots and equipment, there was st᠁ ᠁om for the children to play there when they pleased. Sometimes there were a dozen of them packed together in the small space between our cots and the door. The absence of children of our own made the Pilagá youngsters realize that there was no basic reason for the exclusion of them in favor of someone else. The fact that we lived alone in our hut, and not like the Pilagá in a multiple familied long house, removed us from the hostilities that develop among neighbors and keep them apart. And, since we had no real kinship ties to any one child, we were potential relatives of all of them. Hence we could be uncle, mother, or older sibling to all the children at once.

A word is necessary about children's games. Many primitive cultures, the Pilagá among them, have children's games that are as highly standardized as are "London Bridge" or "Prisoner's Base" in our culture. But for every formalized type of play in a culture there may be a dozen unformalized types. When children in our culture are leaping in and out of a ditch, wading in a brook, or rolling on the ground in rough-and-tumble, they are playing just as certainly as when they choose sides for baseball or hockey. It would seem superfluous and even presumptuous to mention this were it not for the fact that so many anthropological monographs list only the formalized games of children and ignore all the spontaneous and unstructuralized play. Our experience has been that Pilagá children express much more of themselves in unformalized play than in the other type. It must not be imagined, however, that unformalized play is *unpatterned* play. Unstructuralized play is patterned by culturally determined psychic processes that compel the same repetitions of play form day after day.

The problem of physical contact with the children must always be faced at some time during a field trip. Pilagá children are fond of bodily contact with adults and with each other. They frequently press themselves against adults. This attitude was a valuable asset in our field work. In other cultures, however, physical contact may result in the development of special attitudes in the children that might in the end be harmful to the field work. It is clear that the ethnologist must decide for himself exactly what the situation is.

One who intends to make an intimate study of children cannot expect to keep clean. Among the Pilagá work with the children would have been unthinkable on such a basis. We would emerge from our tent in the morning radiant in clean khaki or denim, and in half an hour would be dirty from head to foot after one or two children, covered with a mixture of mud, fruit juices, and charcoal, had clambered all over us. But that is child life —and it is hard to study it without getting some of it on one's clothes.[5]

The problem of the study of primitive children is a formidable one. The language is strange; the culture is strange; children, even in our own culture difficult for adults to approach, seem doubly so in a strange culture. Besides, the time the ethnologist has in the field rarely extends over a year —it is not everyone who can be so fortunate as the field workers in the American Southwest who can return to their people year after year to renew their observations. Confronted with these problems, the conscientious anthropologist is very likely to despair—often quite articulately —of the possibilities of obtaining an intimate knowledge of a group of primitive children. This presentation is, in part, an attempt to show that such despair is premature. To study children in any culture, *it is simply necessary to devote one's time to them*. It is natural that the ethnologist who is concerned with the details of culture—with gardening, canoe-building, ceremonial, and kinship—will have very little time for children. So they will flit past him, mysterious little brown or yellow beings, absorbed in their own concerns, aloof from this adult who is quite naturally occupied with adult affairs. In our work among the Pilagá, however, our time was fairly evenly divided between children and adults, and the children ceased to be mysterious. When two people cooperate in field work the time devoted to children does not result in the impoverishment of the data obtained on other aspects of the culture.

A great barrier to familiarity with children is the language. Not a few ethnologists still maintain that primitive languages cannot be learned quickly enough to be of service in intimate communication—whether with children or adults—in a year's field trip. We hope that this work will be an answer to them.[6] None of the adult Pilagá spoke enough Spanish to make communication in that language worth while, and the children knew no Spanish at all. After six months, however, we were fairly well versed in the Pilagá language, and by the time we were ready to leave we were almost fluent.

Although through Franz Boas and Hans Uldall, Jules Henry had the benefit of extensive linguistic training, Zunia Henry had none. Yet, working side by side, we both learned to talk the Pilagá language almost equally

---

[5] It is obvious that where children have skin or other contagious diseases they must be avoided.
[6] Those interested in the linguistic problem may consult Henry (3) (4) (5).

well, though it is an extremely difficult language. Although the verb has no tenses and maintains a constant form in the singular, the plural bursts forth in an incredible exuberance of complexity. There are a few rules, but they are complicated and abound in exceptions. The same is true of the noun. In addition, the pronominal prefixes are also irregular. The principal grammatical process is suffixing, and there is a great abundance of suffixes. Often they are extremely general in meaning and react upon the internal form of the stem. The vocabulary is extraordinarily rich and abounds in synonyms and symbolic expressions. All nouns are masculine or feminine gender. Phonetically the language is subtle: words change their meaning according to the length or pitch of a vowel, and the speech of women differs in some respects from that of the men. On the other hand, the language is a pleasant one, and prayers, sometimes recited in blank verse, are melodiously beautiful.

The greatest obstacle in the study of primitive children is the amount of time that must be spent in analysis of the cultural totality. Religious ideas, social organization, subsistence, must all be studied carefully, for child life becomes intelligible only against the background of such cultural realities. It may be impossible for even two people to gain an intimate knowledge of a very complex culture within a year. Fortunately Pilagá culture is very simple.

II. FIELD DATA

PILAGÁ CULTURE[1]

THE Pilagá Indians live near the Pilcomayo River in the Argentine Gran Chaco. Although they have a few small gardens, they depend for most of their food on wild fruits and fish. For about three months of the year, when these are very scarce, they suffer almost semi-starvation.

The Pilagá live in small villages between which there are strong feelings of hostility and fear of sorcery. The population of our village was 127, of whom 37 were children under 15 years of age. The eight houses of the village were arranged round a central plaza which was used for drying fruit, as a playground for children, and for social gatherings.

Almost as soon as one enters a Pilagá village one becomes aware of the children, for they are extremely violent and quarrelsome, and they are hungry for attention. Since, from the etiological point of view, a discussion of home environment throws most light on such problems, we shall begin this discussion with an analysis of the Pilagá household.

The Household. The Pilagá think of their villages and households as groups of blood relatives living together in peace and harmony and supporting one another in all things. Actually, village and household are made up only in part of blood relatives; villagers and housemates do not support one another in all things, and peace and harmony are maintained in the face of tension and repressed hostility.

Although Pilagá housemates call one another by relationship terms, detailed genealogical analysis of household populations shows that as many as half the members of any one household may not be relatives within the strict genealogical definition of the term. They are people who, having been brought together by a variety of circumstances,[2] feel they are related and even use relationship terms for one another, but among whom there is very little solidarity. In some primitive societies solidarity is strengthened through participation by the people in large ceremonies which are for the common good, or in some economic enterprise in which the total yield is pooled. But among the Pilagá there are no ceremonies for the common good, and even where a number of people engage in a joint

---

[1] The discussion of Pilagá culture is reprinted from Henry (2).

[2] The factors most powerful in establishing these agglomerates are: 1) actual relationship; 2) arrival of individuals to join married-in siblings; 3) scattering of village populations due to village decomposition upon the death of a chief.

enterprise, such as communal fishing or food-gathering, there is no pooling of the yield.

Although the Pilagá live in large households containing many families, the basic cooperating unit is still the simple family, and it is this unit that holds food as private property. Some South American Indian tribes, that live in "big houses" sheltering many families, have communal meals in which the large households eat together and share all food, but among the Pilagá each family eats separately at its own hearth.[3] Although people distribute most of the food they obtain by their own work to other members of the household, the primary sanction for giving is not praise or expectation of return, but fear—fear of being called stingy, fear of being left alone, and fear of sorcery.[4] In times of scarcity invitations are hardly ever extended to share "pot-luck." The only expedient open to a hungry person is begging, and begging is humiliating and accompanied by fear of giving offense.

Anywhere in times of scarcity the problem arises as to who is to get what there is. In many societies this situation is met by some system whereby certain relatives, such as an uncle or cousin, for example, are the people traditionally accepted as the ones to receive what there is. But among the Pilagá there is no such system. There is only the idea that everything must be shared among all relatives[5] and, since frequently no account is taken of the fact that there may not be enough to go around, considerable resentment is engendered.

Thus there develop within Pilagá society two closely related cycles of feeling which produce great tension and hostility.[6] The first cycle is: reluctance to share is accompanied by reluctance to beg. Reluctance to beg leads to exclusion from sharing, which produces resentment and, in turn, leads to reluctance to share. The second cycle develops in part from the physical fact of scarcity and the inefficient mechanism for distribution. These result in exclusion from sharing, which again produces resentment. In this way Pilagá customs of food distribution strengthen hostility to a degree rare among primitive societies.

[3] Frequently, in times of scarcity, a family with food places its pot in a conspicuous place—usually outside the house—as a tacit invitation to the less fortunate. This, however, is not a "true invitation" and is accepted with reluctance. True invitations are rarely given. A true invitation is a shout to the guest or a visit to his house by the host in order to fetch him.

[4] One who gives also receives from others, but food is also given away to those from whom returns are neither expected nor received.

[5] I speak here of relationship in the broadest sense as conceived by the Pilagá.

[6] Actual outbursts are rare, and it is this fact of repression that aggravates the situation, not only from the psychological but also from the legal point of view, for if the withholding person were roundly insulted he would hesitate before being stingy.

The Cultural Position of Pilagá Women. Although the general lack of dependability and warmth within the household would in any case furnish a very unsatisfactory environment for children, the total situation is made even more difficult because the status of Pilagá women is in so many ways inferior to that of the men.

The women provide only the wild fruits, while the men supply the much more highly valued fish, game and cultivated vegetables. Economically, therefore, women are contemptible to the Pilagá.[7] Women are considered "weak things" and female infanticide was practiced until about ten years ago. Even today when a female child is born its mother may be anxious lest the father ask to have it killed. Women's disabilities, however, extend even further, for status and achievement are not measured in terms of things that women can do. The most desirable wealth is not pots and ponchos—objects of female manufacture—but live-stock, which were obtained in war, and articles of White manufacture.[8]

Pilagá women are even deprived of whatever consideration they might receive as child-bearers, for it is believed that the man's ejaculation projects a complete homunculus into the woman, and that it merely grows in her until it is big enough to come out.

Finally, the woman has no part in that which above all things is the way to prestige in Pilagá culture—warfare. The women show considerable hostility to the men and say the men are "no good." In the courting dances the women have the upper hand and maltreat the men unmercifully. By tradition the woman picks her partner and he will be her lover for the night. Since there are few women and many men,[9] the men must wait patiently and endure all. The women beat the men and jerk them around by the hair violently enough almost to throw them.

Marriage Arrangements. The environment which is rendered difficult for children by the lack of solidarity among the members of the household and by the special disabilities of women is made still worse by Pilagá marriage regulations.

---

[7] During the summer months the older men are drunk almost continuously on beer made from the wild fruits which the women provide. Yet, although the women obediently go for many gallons of water to make this beer, often walking miles to get it, and provide the firewood to heat it, they do not touch a drop of it. *Mate*, too, is largely consumed by the men. Although the women love tobacco, generally the only time they get a chance to smoke is when the ethnologist gives them some tobacco.

[8] Nowadays these things can be obtained by working for Whites part of the year, but since an Indian woman receives only half the pay of a man, the old pattern is perpetuated.

[9] The general numerical superiority of the men is increased by the women's reluctance to dance for fear of the men and of the hordes of violent little boys who attack them.

Because of incest taboos a woman usually chooses her husband from a different village. He is thus an outsider. This arrangement whereby a man leaves his own village in order to live among his wife's people is called matrilocal residence in anthropological parlance, and in many primitive societies where it exists it operates to give maximum security to the woman while cutting the ground from under the man. This occurs most frequently where there is great solidarity between the girl and her group and where she and her group hold all the rights in the land.[10] Among the Pilagá, however, where there is no great solidarity among members of the same household and village, and where the rights in a few little patches of land are held only by the few older men who care to trouble themselves with gardening, the situation is reversed. Far from being in any way dependent on their wives' kin, husbands are great assets to the household, for they take the place of the young men who marry out and they provide the highly valued animal foods. The wife has no property rights of any importance[11] and no great personal backing in her own village. So, too, the woman becomes particularly dependent on her husband because he is one of the few people from whom she can take food and property without fear of his resentment.

What actually happens in Pilagá society is that both husband and wife show rather extreme signs of insecurity.[12] To a young husband his wife's village, like most villages other than his own, is one toward which he has always had a marked conscious hostility, and the men and women of strange villages are always felt to be sorcerers. For months after he has entered his wife's village the husband is scarcely visible. At the crack of dawn he is off to his mother's house, if it is not too far away, and he only returns to his wife at night. If he remains with his wife during the day he often stays indoors, lying down.

Pilagá wives, on the other hand, tell many stories of husbands who beat their wives[13] when they find them visiting even in another part of the same household. If a group of gossiping women detects a distant movement in the bush they are in a mild panic of fear of their husbands and scuttle back to their fires. Over and over again the women warned Mrs. Henry to run home when they saw J. Henry coming in the distance. "Go! Run! He'll beat

---

[10] Or in some other important property.

[11] She owns only her personal belongings.

[12] The extreme symptoms of the man wear off in the course of a year.

[13] Once a child has been born to him a man begins to take a more active part in village life. Nevertheless he still spends most of his time in his wife's section of the house. Women never lose their fear of being beaten for visiting.

you!" It made no difference to them that she assured them that he was not "fierce" and that he never beat her.

In our society important motivating forces behind marriage are love and economic advantage. Among the Pilagá, however, emotional bonds do not play a very important role, and in early youth economic considerations do not loom large. Certain factors do, however, make marriage desirable to the young people. Although the unmarried women in a household will fetch water for a young man and provide him with vegetable food and even with some firewood, once the women are married the products of their labor go to their husbands and children, and the unmarried young men become increasingly uncomfortable. Although there is premarital sexual freedom, the young men are eager to marry because, since they outnumber the young women, they find it difficult to obtain sexual partners. Young women, on the other hand, never lack for lovers and are not so eager to marry as the young men. Yet ultimately they must marry in order to avoid becoming beggars.[14]

The lack of large economic stakes on both sides, however, and the absence of deep emotional attachments make early marriage so unstable that it has about it very much the air of a casual affair. Since no Pilagá child can be born without a father, the pregnancies resulting from these unions must be aborted.[15] Among the young women abortions and threats of abortion are so frequent that one could almost say of a first child that it is just an unperformed abortion.

Thus far the examination of Pilagá institutions has shown: 1) that the household fails to provide adequate security; 2) that food sharing, the mechanism for insuring solidarity among individuals, develops considerable tension among them; 3) that women suffer important disabilities; 4) that marriage itself contributes to the emotional insecurity of both husband and wife; and 5) that the great instability of early marriages acts as a constant threat to early pregnancies. Still other disturbing factors develop from situations that are correlated with pregnancy and lactation rules.

Pregnancy and Lactation. Traditionally, a Pilagá woman must go to her husband's village[16] as soon as she becomes pregnant, and the husband takes this opportunity to demand that she go there. This may precipitate

[14] Parental pressure is important too, for the parents want the husband as a fisherman.

[15] The Pilagá have no contraceptive techniques.

[16] She may never return to her own village, or she may return after her child is born or even sooner.

a severe conflict, for now it is the girl's turn to be afraid of the sorcerers in her husband's village.

Nenarachí, our next-door neighbor, is a case in point. When she became pregnant her husband made the usual demand—that she follow him to his village. For a long time she refused until he at last beat her. Next day she went with him. When we went to visit her in her husband's village, the change that had come over her was shocking. When we saw her there the first time she was watching a tattooing. Now, since women are the tattooers, a tattooing is an event which is always of the greatest interest to them. They watch the work with expert eye and laugh and talk a great deal. Not so Nenarachí. She sat stony and sad. When Mrs. Henry asked whether she was happy in her husband's village she whispered, "No. I will never be happy here." She was afraid of sorcerers and told Mrs. Henry so. About six weeks later she left her husband, and we were delighted one morning to see Nenarachí back in our village.

But now there was talk of an abortion. "Who would take care of the child?" said the Pilagá. So for a week or so there were rumors that Nenarachí was going to "throw away her child," but at last one night her husband returned. He told us that his relatives had insisted that he come back so that the "child would not be killed." Thus the conflict arising out of residence rules for the pregnant woman may result in a threat to the life of the child. As time goes on and second and third children are born Pilagá marriages become more stable. Nevertheless there is still another factor that acts as a constant threat to marital relationships and makes the position of the mother particularly difficult.

From the time she is six months pregnant until her baby can run about sexual intercourse is taboo to the Pilagá mother, for the Pilagá believe that were a woman to have intercourse when she was "big" the child in her womb would die; and if she were to give birth to a second child before the first could run about then the first child would die. The women will not nurse two of their own children at once, and they believe that if a child is weaned before it can run about it will not eat.

A long taboo on intercourse during pregnancy and lactation is found in many parts of the primitive world. In many cultures where it occurs, however, the difficulties arising from it are solved through the institution of polygyny. The Pilagá woman, however, will not tolerate a co-wife. An important factor in female opposition to a co-wife may be seen in the matrilocal residence rule. Since the small population of Pilagá villages makes it very unlikely that a man could find two wives in one village, he would have to divide his time, and hence his contributions of food and game, between two villages. As a matter of fact, although polygyny among the Pilagá is rare, in the few cases that do occur, the wives are, with rare exception, in separate villages. Even were it possible for a man to find two wives in one village his contributions would most likely be divided between two families—all the more so since female infanticide makes it very unlikely that two marriageable sisters could be found in one household. When, in addition to these factors, we consider the lack of solidarity between Pilagá households, it becomes clear that the whole idea of a co-wife must be intolerable to a Pilagá woman.[17] Therefore, although she may be willing to let her husband have affairs, she will fight both her husband and the other woman if an affair becomes serious.

Factors Affecting the Desirability of Children. The Pilagá woman occupies an inferior position in her culture and, like her husband, she is reared in an atmosphere of insecurity and tension. This tension is heightened by fear of her husband and by the anxiety which the taboo on intercourse injects into her life. Her marriage represents to her the sacrifice of her freedom to economic necessity.

For the young wife a first child is at least a partial guarantee of economic security, for pressure is brought to bear to keep the couple together in order to preserve the child. To all women, however, a baby is equally a threat, for the taboo on intercourse sends their husbands out in search of adventure. Finally, infants interfere with their mothers' work, and not only do some women object to having children because of it, but actually contemplate abortions.[18]

To the young husband the baby represents his most secure tie to his wife, and at all times it is evidence of a man's "good work," for he alone is responsible for its being. So too, once a child is born to him a man's marriage has more the appearance of a stable union and he begins to acquire status in his wife's village. On the other hand the presence of the baby means a taboo on intercourse and some men say, although none too seriously, that they are jealous of their newborn infants. Thus a number of cultural factors operate to make babies both desirable and undesirable.

The Development of the Child's Personality. Thus far the discussion of Pilagá institutions has shown that there are a great number of factors

---

[17] The preponderance of males over females is another factor that makes polygyny difficult.

[18] We have no instances of the abortion of a second pregnancy in a married woman living with her husband.

making for insecurity, and that although a child is to a certain extent desirable, in many cases the desire is far from whole-hearted. When the baby
at last comes into the world it is received with great warmth, but as time
passes it is gradually rejected. The initial warmth is followed by gradual
withdrawal, until by the time the third sibling is born the first gets practically no attention at all beyond receiving the necessities of life.

When the baby is young it is the object of constant attention. At the
first whimper it is nursed by its mother, or in her absence, sometimes by
its grandmother. It is bathed and kept free of lice, and its mother carefully
plucks out its eyelashes to make it beautiful. She kisses it over and over
again, rubbing her mouth violently on the baby's in an ecstasy of pleasure.
The baby is passed around from hand to hand and people in the house and
visitors take turns mouthing it. But as time passes, as the baby's personality begins to develop, and as the baby becomes more and more interested
in the things around it, it gets less and less attention from everyone, for
the adults regard the child's expanding interests as rejection.

The withdrawal of attention takes place by almost imperceptible degrees, and is evident at first only in the mother's increased slowness in
stopping her work to nurse her weeping baby, and in diminished mouth
rubbing.

At about the eighth month of the infant's life two important factors
operate with particular vigor to undermine the child's security. These
factors are his mother's work and the absence of solidarity within the
household. In order to gather in the crops of wild fruits the child's mother
must spend hours away from home. She often cannot take the child with
her, for the distance she has to go is too great and the baby too heavy to
carry in addition to her burden of wild fruit. In some primitive communi-
ties where similar conditions exist the mother can leave her child with
some other woman who will suckle it if it grows hungry or weeps. Among
the Pilagá, however, this does not often occur because there is so little
solidarity within the household and because the reluctance to take food
from others forces all the able-bodied women and many of the weak and
aged to go out to look for food. Often, therefore, the baby is left with an
old and feeble (sometimes blind)[19] grandparent who can do little for it.

The period of greatest suffering for the baby begins, however, when it
can walk a little. This is the time when it begins to explore the world outside the house.[20] Alone, outside the familiar circle of its housemates, the

---

[19] In our village there were five totally blind individuals—all old people.
[20] The babies are often encouraged by their mothers to go outside.

child is afraid. Little children tear past at breakneck speed, screaming, or tumble about on the ground in violent play. Strangers walk by. The baby bursts into tears, but its elders are slow to reassure it.

During the period when the baby is investigating the outer world it is almost continuously in tears. Not only is it frightened by contact with strangers, but its mother leaves it more and more alone as she goes about her work. Formerly she had left the baby alone for hours; now she leaves him alone for a whole day. He eats a little pounded corn or drinks a little honey water, but the baby is hungry, and by evening is so wrought up that when the tired mother comes home, he often cannot wait to be picked up, but has a tantrum at her feet.

Although as the Pilagá child grows older he receives the breast less often, partly because he eats other things, partly because he is busy playing, and often because his mother is away working, he can still have access to her breast frequently. He is still very much the object of his mother's attention, and he spends many hours sitting on her thighs as she parts his hair looking for lice. Once a new sibling appears, however, this is radically changed. Though his mother may nurse him even while she is in labor, when the child is born the older sibling is absolutely denied the breast. Not only this, but the attention his mother and father once gave him is now directed to the new baby. Formerly when he wept he was given the breast and comforted by his mother. Now he is told to "be quiet" and sent to play outdoors or to a relative who may afford him some casual comfort in the form of a morsel of food.

This situation leaves the older sibling stunned. He wanders disconsolately about near the house and whimpers continually, apparently without cause. When he comes home it is not infrequently to try out little schemes for doing away with the new baby, and his mother must be very watchful lest he injure the new sibling. Naturally this only intensifies the situation, for the mother's redoubled attention serves to isolate the older sibling even more.

In some cultures the shock of rejection may be somewhat lessened through a marked change in the status of the older sibling, or through some device whereby he is given considerable prestige or made to feel important. In other cultures, again, the older sibling becomes the care of some special relative who takes the child everywhere and is a constant companion. Among the Pilagá, however, these things do not occur. The Pilagá have no device for giving status or prestige to anyone below the rank of chief, and one of the outstanding facts of Pilagá life is that no one troubles himself much about a child with a younger sibling. In view of the foregoing discussion of Pilagá social structure we can readily understand why no one other than the parents should bother much about the child, but why fathers should show such indifference is another matter. It is not that all Pilagá fathers are completely indifferent to the child who has just been weaned. Indeed, some fathers take them visiting, buy them gifts, and even delouse them. But their interest in the child never extends to the play and fondling that is typical of the responsive father in our society. Over and over again among the Pilagá the picture is of the apathetic father who suffers his little child to squat between his knees. As we have seen, there is good reason, in the social arrangements in this tribe, for the jealousy of their infants which Pilagá fathers explicitly remark upon, and warmth does not develop between fathers and children.

Thus, without status and deprived of warmth, the child remains a poor hostile little flounderer for a number of years until he at last begins to take his place in the adult economic activity.

DRAMATIS PERSONNAE

This is not a house census but merely a list of the people whose names appear in this paper.

HOUSE I

Name	Age	Sex	Description
Sidingkí	50 yrs.	M	Father of Nenarachí, Yalakachítn, and Naichó
Yalákachitn	30	F	
Nenarachí	25	F	
Naichó	6	F	
Sutaráina	75	F	Mother of Sidingkí
Piyarasáina	60	F	Sister of Sutaráina
Waik	65	M	Half-brother of Sidingkí
Diwá'i	35	F	Mother of Tapáñi, Yorodaikolík, and Denikí
Tapáñi	9	F	
Yorodaikolík		M	
Denikí	15 mos.	M	
Nagête	40	F	Mother of Araná
Araná	25	F	
Lawésakachiyi	6	M	

HOUSE II

Name	Age	Sex	Description
Simíti	10	F	Sister of Dañakána
Dañakána	6	F	
Lorosétina	23	F	Sister of Kayolí and Kapíetn
Kayolí	8	F	
Kapíetn	3½	M	

HOUSE III

Name	Age	Sex	Description
Kaláchiyoli	40	F	Cousin by marriage of Sorói
Ñorol'í	60	F	Mother of Kaláchiyolí
Sorói	7	F	

HOUSE IV

Name	Age	Sex	Description
Suvyaraikítn	15	M	
Chaupá	12–13	F	Sister of Kanaidí, Darotoyí, and Simkoolí
Kanaidí	9½	M	
Darotoyí	4	M	
Simkoolí	1	F	

DRAMATIS PERSONNAE—*Continued*

House V

Name	Age	Sex	Description
Katinorodí	10	M	Brother of Kuwasiñítn
Kuwasiñítn	8	M	
Maralú	12	M	Half-brother of Wetél
Wetél	6	M	
Tanorow'í	10	F	
Ñakéte	9	F	Sister of Mátakana and Hetolí
Mátakana	3	F	
Hetolí	15 mos.	M	

House VI

Oma'í	40	M	Father of Nakínak and Adíechi
Nakínak	6	M	
Adíechi	8	M	Half-brother of Nakínak

House VII

Later Tanorow'í, Ñakéte, Mátakana, and Hetolí moved into this house.

House VIII

Anetolí	9	F	Sister of Yatákana
Yatákana	5	F	

FIELD OBSERVATION OF SIBLING RIVALRY

Introduction. Sibling rivalry is a characteristic feature of Pilagá familial relationships, and what might perhaps be called the "simple sibling rivalry situation"—direct hostility toward the younger sibling because of displacement—emerges with great clarity in real life in the culture and in the experimental play with dolls. In families in which there are several siblings, however, the conditions are complex, and where the Oedipus situation enters the entire conflict may be displaced in a different direction. Thus, much of the conflict between Simíti and her younger sister Dañakána revolved about their competition for their father on a straightforward sexual basis. In other cases the hostility may be pushed in a particular direction because of special determining causes, particularly where the parents take an active part in the control and direction of hostility. Thus, in the case of the three siblings Tapáñi, Yorodaikolík, and Denikí, the conflict between Yorodaikolík and his baby brother Denikí was nowhere nearly as sharp as between both of these children and their elder sister Tapáñi. Because of her personality disturbances and her ugliness, Tapáñi was the village scapegoat. The mother stimulated the two younger children to attack Tapáñi, whom she detested. Tapáñi, *on the other hand, entertained much more serious hostility to her mother than to her siblings.

Guilt. In spite of complicating factors, sibling rivalry based on displacement may be detected in almost every case in which there is a younger sibling. The accompanying behavior patterns, however, are somewhat different from those in our culture. This is due in part to a difference in moral ideas and sentiments between the two cultures. Among the Pilagá there is no strong sense of guilt and no institutional support for guilt feelings. This does not mean that they do not experience guilt feelings, but rather that those feelings are different in some respects from what is experienced in our culture. An understanding of guilt in our culture is impossible without taking into consideration the feelings of remorse and loss of self-esteem which are so often part of it. Among the Pilagá, however, there is little of this. The daily experience of Pilagá children is not remorse or loss of self-esteem, but fear of retaliation. Self-punishment and self-accusation imply feelings of remorse, and they loom large in the Levy sibling rivalry experiments. *Self-punishment and self-accusation do not occur in any of the Pilagá material.*

* Tapáñi and Yorodaikolík are discussed in detail in Henry (6) and (7).

In this connection it is interesting to observe that the Pilagá tell only one story of suicide; but the suicide itself only serves to emphasize again the absence of the remorse and loss of self-esteem components in the Pilagá guilt complex. The story—a true one—is that a certain man had murdered three of his tribesmates, and that his relatives had become so disgusted with him that they asked him to kill himself. He did so by shooting himself. In this case the individual is forced into self-punishment, not by his own feeling of remorse, but by the direct action of his outraged tribesmen.

In our culture the feelings of remorse and loss of self-esteem that are so often components of guilt weigh upon the individual at least as heavily as the fear of retaliation, and extend to many aspects of his life. This may be responsible in great part for the self-punishment in Levy's cases. People in our culture "feel guilty" for all kinds of things, big and little: the professor feels guilty because he has not written to a former student; Mrs. Jones feels guilty because she forgot to send a wedding anniversary greeting to her former maid; Mr. Doe feels guilty because he has divorced his faithful wife for a beautiful blonde. But the whole complicated apparatus of guilt—what ethnologists would call the institutional support for guilt—extending from church to sports in our culture, is missing among the Pilagá. They have no penitent speeches and no confessional. Self-flagellation does not occur and they are strangers to "gentlemen's codes of honor."

In studying the Pilagá child's behavior toward his peers it is also important to consider the relevant love attitudes. Sibling love is not a trait for which a Pilagá child obtains the approval of his parents. The rewards for sibling love are *nil;* the punishment for sibling injury is mild and uncertain. Hence, it is not uncommon for a Pilagá child to detest his younger sibling and he does not attempt to conceal it. The attitudes toward parents are also different among the Pilagá than among ourselves. The atmosphere of sanctity, impeccability, and compulsory love with which parents in our culture surround themselves is missing among the Pilagá. Pilagá parents are much more the equals of their children. They do not demand absolute love, honor, and respect as do parents in our culture, nor do they drill into their children the "Oh, how much I have suffered for you" theme. If an angry Pilagá child hesitates to insult his erring parent, it is not for fear of disturbing some cloud-enveloped holiness, but rather to avoid a blow or a dousing with cold water. All of these contrasting attitudes should be borne in mind when considering the Pilagá material.

Field observation of sibling rivalry among the Pilagá has produced no evidence of self-accusation or self-defense. In as much as those factors do not appear in the experimental material either, they may be said to be missing from the sibling rivalry syndrome among the Pilagá. Restitution, another factor in the guilt complex associated with sibling rivalry in our culture, does occur in theirs. This type of behavior has been described by Levy[21] as "activities that restore or attempt to restore the attacked objects to their original state." The following are some examples from Pilagá culture:

Denikí hits Darotoyí who hits him back and then gives him a piece of tin.

Kanaidí throws down his brother Darotoyí. Darotoyí screams, and Kanaidí goes up to him to comfort him.

Kapíetn, for no visible reason, makes a dive for his sister Kayolí and she hits him. He screeches. She smiles. When he goes toward home she follows him and tries to pick him up. He throws himself down in a tantrum. She picks him up and carries him into their house. She gives him fruit and he stops crying.

When the anthropologist puts an arm around Kapíetn, his sister Kayolí immediately strikes him in the face. He starts to cry and she tries to comfort him by pulling his head against her.

The following examples show a certain amount of discomfort on the part of the offending child:

Yorodaikolík drops some bits of cheese we had given him. Kanái'i (not a sibling) snatches one and runs away. Yorodaikolík looks terribly pained and bursts into tears. Naichó (not a sibling) looks angry and points out Kanái'i. Kanái'i *looks guilty* and gives cheese to Yorodaikolík.

Maralú's brother Wetél is standing in front of him after a free-for-all for pieces of cabbage. Maralú says to Wetél, "Begging!" and kicks him. When Wetél starts to cry Maralú *looks embarrassed* and pulls Wetél toward him in a comforting gesture, and sets him down. Wetél stops crying. The kick was not a hard one.

Chaupá takes away Darotoyí's basin of fruit. He starts to cry, and follows her to get his basin back. She gives him the basin, but he dumps the contents on the ground and throws the basin away. She picks up the basin and goes home, *looking disturbed*. Darotoyí stands there weeping.

It is interesting to see the range of variation in the interpretation of facial expression. It is probable that "disturbed" is the safest of the three terms used.

Adult attitudes toward a given form of behavior are important in the

[21] Op. cit., p. 57.

development of children's attitudes toward that behavior. Pilagá adults, however, are little concerned with child violence.

Ponaradí, age three, strikes a younger child, who cries and runs to its mother. Lisorodítn (a much older boy) calls out to Ponaradí, "Why did you hit him? Are you a fool?" Here ZH has a very significant note: "This is the first time I ever heard or saw an offending child scolded," after seven months in the field. The note refers, of course, to incidents of this type.[22]

As a matter of fact, it is impossible to predict whether a violent child will be scolded by the parent or relative of the child he has attacked, or whether the injured child will himself be scolded by his parents or relatives for weeping. Often it is the latter.

Tapáñi is watching her mother nurse the baby and play with Yorodaikolík, her younger sibling. Suddenly she strikes Yorodaikolík, who has climbed on the mother's shoulder. When he bursts into tears his mother says to him, "Stop, or you'll be left here when we go to the fish trap." She says nothing at all to Tapáñi and does not even frown at her.

Darotoyí, a little boy neighbor, makes Yorodaikolík weep. Nagête (housemate and relative of Yorodaikolík) calls out, "Yorodaikolík will be tied up!"

This type of behavior at times expresses the unwillingness of adults to provoke further dissension by siding with one child or the other, but it expresses also the fundamental lack of solidarity within the Pilagá relationship group.

The most powerful control of violence within the child world is the punishment administered by the children themselves. This is mostly insult, scolding, and physical violence.

Symmetrical and Reciprocal Hostility. The problem of sibling rivalry in our culture has been phrased almost exclusively in terms of the hostility of the older sibling to the younger one, who has displaced him in the mother's attentions.[23] Discussions of sibling rivalry have revolved about the loss, or the fear of loss, of the mother by the older sibling. The rivalry situation has been viewed in terms of the desire of the older sibling to destroy the younger, and thus claim the mother exclusively as his own. In this connection, however, the question naturally arises as to what the attitude of the younger sibling is. If his older sibling resents his intrusion, does the younger one return the compliment? Is the younger

---

[22] This was recorded in a different village. Hence the names do not appear among the Dramatis Personnae.

[23] The points developed in the following paragraphs have been elaborated in Henry (8.)

sibling as much in fear of the competition[24] of the older as the latter is of the competition of the younger?

It is difficult to believe that the younger sibling is passive before the onslaughts of his older brother or sister.[25] It is also difficult to believe that in a culture which gives rise to competitive attitudes between siblings the competition developing around the mother should not be present very early in the younger as well as in the older sibling. It seems probable that where competition develops around the mother, the attitudes of the siblings should be *symmetrical*.[26]

The problem thus defined requires two types of evidence for its solution: 1) material showing the resentment by the younger of the intrusion of the older; 2) material showing that where the older sibling is hostile to the younger, the latter *reciprocates*. Fortunately both types are available from our field notes.

1. MATERIAL SHOWING THE RESENTMENT BY THE YOUNGER OF THE INTRUSION OF THE OLDER

a) Yoradaikolík (male, age 4) is weeping because, say the children, his brother, Denikí, age 15 months, hit him. Denikí is *kalawaráik*, violent, they say. Yoradaikolík goes home and his mother extends her hand to him. When he goes to her she wipes his face. Denikí hits his mother and throws himself downward and backward in a typical Pilagá baby tantrum. The mother washes Yorodaikolík's face and he becomes quiet. When she is finished she picks up Denikí, who is still lying down weeping. When she washes his face he screeches. Then she nurses him and he immediately becomes quiet.

b) The mother is delousing Yorodaikolík. Denikí bites her arm when he does not get attention. Then she nurses him, but he tries to pull her arm away from Yorodaikolík.

c) Kanaidí's mother comes to visit us. She sits down in front of the tent and calls Kanaidí (male, age 9 years 6 months), to sit beside her. She delouses him. She has brought along her year old daughter Simkoolí.

---

[24] In Mead, M. (2), competition is defined as "the act of seeking or endeavoring to gain what another is endeavoring to gain at the same time" (p. 8). On p. 17 it is pointed out that whereas competition is "behavior oriented toward a goal in which the other competitors for that goal are secondary, rivalry is behavior oriented toward another human being, whose worsting is the primary goal, and the object or position for which they compete is secondary."

[25] Levy (op. cit.) has shown experimentally that for many hostile acts against mother and baby there is some form of self-retaliatory behavior.

[26] For the theoretical concepts underlying this discussion we are indebted to Bateson, G. (1). We have, however, been rather less rigorous in the use of his terminology than he might be.

Simkoolí sits on a box and seems quite contented, but as soon as her mother starts to delouse Kanaidí, Simkoolí calls to her mother and pushes Kanaidí. He gently restrains her. She almost falls and seizes his nose and holds on. Kanaidí laughs and puts her back on the box. She keeps trying to get her mother's attention all the time. At last Kanaidí gets up and leaves.

2. Material Showing That Where the Older Sibling Is Hostile to the Younger, the Latter Reciprocates

Where the older sibling is hostile to the younger it is not always easy to see the younger sibling's revenge, because the difference in strength at times makes the enterprise perilous for the weaker one. Nevertheless the younger can be seen at times to take things into his own hands, as in the following examples.

a) Deniki goes to Yorodaikolík who is looking at one of our picture books. Yorodaikolík regards Deniki with a look of hatred, but permits him to examine the book with him. When Yorodaikolík moves away Deniki follows him. As Yorodaikolík sits there Deniki bangs him on the head a number of times.

b) Yorodaikolík snatches at Deniki's penis. Their mother is looking at a picture book. When Yorodaikolík reaches for it the ethnologist gives it to him, but Deniki shows that he wants it. Yorodaikolík shuts the book and holds on to it. Deniki weeps and hits Yorodaikolík in the face. The mother nurses Deniki.

c) Yorodaikolík starts to weep because he is thirsty, and suddenly, for no ostensible reason, slaps Deniki who is looking at some pictures. Deniki regards Yorodaikolík for a moment, looks again at the pictures, and suddenly hits Yorodaikolík.

d) Kanaidí angrily tells his brother Darotoyí, age 4, to go home. He pushes him. Darotoyí bursts into tears. A few moments later Kanaidí repeats: "Go home!" and pounds Darotoyí on the back. Darotoyí tries to throw something. At last Kanaidí throws Darotoyí down and he screams. Kanaidí goes up to him to comfort him.

e) Darotoyí sticks his year-old sister in the breast with a stick. She scratches him. Darotoyí says: "Look, she did this."

If all the children in a Pilagá family compete for the mother the resulting hostility must become ever more intense. If C is the baby and B and A the older siblings, we have a situation something like this: B resents the intrusion of C, and C retaliates as best he can. But B, offended in his turn by the hostility of C, pays him back. Hence the hostility mounts. C, in his turn, resents B's competition for the mother too, and tries to keep him away from her. This gives rise to another cycle of hostility. Meanwhile the old strife between B and A, the oldest of the three, continues. A, however, also objects to the presence of C, and C to the presence of A. Thus, C has to cope with A and B; A must struggle against B and C; and B must withstand A and C. Hence there is a constant, reversible, and clearly perceptible flow of blows from one sibling to another wherever strength permits. In all truth it may be said of a Pilagá baby that he learns to fight almost before he learns to walk.

Relation between sibling rivalry and other factors. Sewall found that siblings "12 to 36 months older than the baby (rival) show a higher frequency of sibling rivalry."[27] The situation among the Pilagá, however, is different, for as between neighboring siblings hostility always exists no matter what the age difference.[28] If all the cases of hostility of children to their next youngest siblings be considered, and the severest cases be selected from among these, we find the following age differences: between Koitaháa and his infant brother there is a difference of about 21–24 months; between Tapáñi and Yorodaikolík and between Kanaidí and Darotoyí there is a difference of about 3–4 years; between Kayolí and Kapíetn there is a difference of about 4–5 years, and between Maralú and Wetél there is a difference of over 5 years. Thus, among the Pilagá the intensity of the hostility does not depend on age differences.

Among the Pilagá we do not find the condition, so common in our society, of rivalry of the younger sibling with the older *on the basis of parental preference for the older*. In our culture the intelligence, beauty, or personality of the older sibling, or his resemblance to one of the parents may result in the concentration of attention on the older sibling to the exclusion of the younger. Such factors have little weight with the Pilagá.[29] They do not make the fine distinctions we do, and although they recognize resemblances to parents when the resemblances are called to their attention, these are of no importance to them. The whole weight of cultural interest is always thrown to the helpless infant. When it is no longer helpless the Pilagá begin to lose interest in it.

In our culture "we see a diminishing percentage of overt rivalry frequencies by the next to the youngest child, with increased size of fami-

---

[27] Levy, op. cit., p. 10.

[28] This seems to be more in conformity with the results obtained by Smalley who found that "jealousy bore no relationship to age difference . . . " (10, p. 467).

[29] A possible exception to this is Tapáñi. She was, however, so ugly and undersized that it was recognized by everyone in the village.

lies."[30] Among the Pilagá, however, size of family has no effect on the development of overt rivalry, nor upon its intensity. In the six cases of intense hostility the number of children in each family was as follows: three families with three children; two with two children, and one with four children. Since the average number of children per family in our village was three, the figures indicate that intensity of hostility is not determined by the number of children in the family. The two cases of least hostility occur in families of two or three children.

TABLE I

INCIDENCE AND INTENSITY OF INTER-SIBLING HOSTILITY

Name	Age	Older					Younger				
		21–24 months	25–36 months	37–48 months	49–60 months	5 years or more	21–24 months	25–36 months	37–48 months	49–60 months	5 years or more
1. Chaupá	12–13							×			×o
2. Kanaidí	9 yrs. 6 mos.		×								×*×
3. Darotoyí	4					×*×		×			
4. Tapáñi	8–9								×*		×
5. Yorodaikolík	4				×*			×			
6. Deniki	15 mos.		×			×					
7. Ñakéte	9								×		?
8. Mátakana	3					?					
9. Kayolí	8					o				×*	
10. Kapíetn	3 yrs. 6 mos.				×*	?					
11. Simíti	10							×			
12. Dañakána	6			×							
13. Anetolí	9					?		×			?
14. Yatákana	5			×		?		×			
15. Maralú	12										×*
16. Wetél	6					×*					
17. Katinorodí	10					?		o			
18. Kuwasiñítn	8		o			?					
19. Naichó	6					××					
20. Sorói	7		?								
21. Lawésakachiyi	6					???					
22. Tanorowí	10					?					
23. Nakínak	6				?				?		
24. Koitaháa	3 or 3 yrs. 6 mos.							×*			

* Indicates intense hostility.

EXPLANATION OF TABLE I

Table I presents the results of direct field observation of sibling rivalry. The children about whom we have little or no information have been omitted. Siblings have been grouped together. The siblings of some of the children included

[30] Levy, op. cit., p. 12.

in the table have been omitted either because they were adults or because for one reason or another the contact between the children and their siblings was so slight as to provide no basis for inclusion in the table. Thus, although we saw something of Nakínak who was from the other end of the village, we saw very little of his baby sibling because she stayed at home with her mother. Sorói's brother was away most of the time and so was Tanorowí's sister. We have not included Naichó's sisters because they are adults.

The question marks indicate that information is incomplete. They appear in the cases of Ñakéte and Mátakana because the older brother has married and left the village. In Kapíetn's case it appears because of lack of information. Anetolí and Yatákana have an adult brother who has married and left the village. Katinorodí and Kuwasiñítn were separated from their brother most of the time because he had gone away to work. The same is true of Sorói and Tanorowí. Lawésakachiyi's brothers were all many years older than he, and he was so completely shut out of their world that it was impossible to gauge his attitude toward them by simple observation. Nakínak's little sister spent all her time with her mother at the far end of the village so we had little opportunity to observe Nakínak together with his sister. His stepbrother lived mostly with a grandmother in another village. Koitaháa's brother was only three days old.

The numerals at the head of the 'older' and 'younger' columns indicate the age-gap between siblings. X indicates that inter-sibling hostility was observed. O indicates that observation of the behavior between the siblings revealed no overt hostility. Thus, Chaupá was observed to be hostile to Kanaidí (X in the 25–36 month 'younger' column) and to Darotoyí (X in the 5 years or more 'younger' column) but not to her baby sister (O in the 5 years or more 'younger' column). The baby sister's name (Simkoolí) does not appear in the 'name' column because, since she was a baby, she could not express hostility much.

In a number of cases (as in that of Chaupá) more symbols appear to the right of a name than there are siblings listed in the name column. This occurs either because not all the siblings were observed, or because some of the siblings were adults, or (as in the case of Chaupá) because one or more of the siblings was too young to express much hostility. In the case of Sorói, her brother was away most of the time and so could not be observed. In the case of Naichó and Lawésakachiyi the siblings were all adults.

III. EXPERIMENTAL DATA

PROCEDURE

In our work isolation with the subject was impossible. The village was so compact that the pulse of village life could be felt from every point, and interruptions were frequent. Our house had a brush and mud roof; the "walls" were of reeds and it was easy to see through them. There was a large hole in one wall. The "door" was a rickety screen that was forever on the verge of falling. The house was at one end of the village plaza, and the entire population lived within about a hundred feet of us. Our nearest neighbors lived about ten feet away, and when the weather grew too hot to sleep indoors and we moved outside, we were practically sharing sleeping quarters with them. In such close quarters privacy was impossible, but although it was a strain on us, it had the advantage of giving easy access to all our neighbors and affording the children almost unlimited access to us. Thus we had an excellent opportunity to observe our subjects.

The physical obstacles to privacy, however, were as nothing compared to the emotional ones. Pilagá children cannot tolerate exclusion, and we almost always had several of them in the house at once. Often two or more manipulated the play material at the same time. The protocols of the experiments often show, therefore, the activity of several children manipulating the material at once. The following short abstract from one protocol will serve as an illustration.

JH puts baby doll to nurse. Wetél says: "Oma'í's penis." Nakínak just sits there and does nothing. Now he puts brother doll on mother doll. Wetél puts brother doll on mother doll. Nakínak takes it off scowling. Wetél puts brother doll on Nakínak doll, then on father doll. Kuwasiñítn says: "Tiny anus." He puts brother doll on father doll, penises touching. In a number of cases it was necessary to make a separate extract of the behavior of each child in order to give an idea of his activity. When several children manipulate the material simultaneously they stimulate one another. We have, therefore, tried to give an idea of the nature of the stimulation. Thus, where child A is playing with dolls representing his own family, and child B comes and manipulates the same material, the extract of A's play may read somewhat as follows. A puts the baby doll to nurse. Now B manipulates the material. The last thing he does is put the mother and father dolls in position of intercourse, saying: "Intercourse." A removes the mother doll and adjusts the breasts, etc.

Under the primitive conditions of the Chaco the ethnologist traveling on a limited budget must dispense with much equipment. Hence we had no play table. Sometimes the children used a packing case, and sometimes a piece of a corrugated paper box laid on the ground. When the children came into our house they saw the following things: two army cots, two chairs, an axe, a large canteen, a large tin used as a supply box, a water pot, a long crate used to house equipment, and a small trunk. They also saw the play box (13″×7″×5″) containing the play material. Since the play material was always visible to several children at once, all of them quickly became familiar with it. Our house was almost as familiar to them as their own houses, for in general the children spent a great deal of time in our house.

The principal play material consisted of the following: 1) A dark brown mother doll made of a paper and plaster composition, seven inches in length, arms and legs slightly bent. The doll can sit but not stand. 2) A father doll. This is the "amputation doll" of David Levy's sibling rivalry experiments, except that it has a universal joint on the back for mounting on a stand. We did not use the stand.[1] The doll is eight inches long, of un-painted metal with painted plaster head, hands, and shoes. The arms and legs are completely jointed and detachable. 3) Several "child" dolls: a) A white "baby" doll three inches long, of celluloid, with arms and legs mov-able at the shoulder and hip. It could sit but not stand. b) A white "older sibling" doll three and one half inches long and made of china. The arms are movable at the shoulder but the legs are rigid. c) Another white "sibling" doll. This celluloid doll was five inches long, with arms movable at the shoulder, but legs rigid.

When more dolls were needed additional "baby" dolls were used. When two children manipulated the material at the same time dolls were some-times added in order to include the siblings of both children.

There were also scissors, a ball of plastiline, and a mechanical turtle operated by means of a string passing through its shell and wound around a revolving wheel. The child moved the turtle by means of the string. If he wished he could direct the turtle's movements. If the turtle was per-mitted to move at random it tended to describe a right angle. When the turtle was first presented to the children, Simíti, who hated Tapáñi, had the turtle strike a doll representing Tapáñi, and said: "It bit Tapáñi." Thereupon the examiner suggested that the turtle bit those it did not like. Throughout the experiments, therefore, the turtle has the character of a

---

[1] In 1936 amputation dolls without the ball on the back could not be obtained in New York.

biting animal. The use of the turtle is not recommended because it makes the release of hostility too easy, and because its movements present difficulties in evaluation. It is also an absorbing toy in itself and may act as a distraction.

The "examiner" is Zunia Henry in every case. Whenever Jules Henry enters the play situation he appears in the protocol as JH. The examiner and JH were in the position of compliant, receptive foster parents or relatives whose sole function was to amuse and accommodate the chilren. The children used kinship terms or our personal names in addressing us.

Play with the dolls was *wholly voluntary*. The children themselves asked to play. The dolls were then given to them and each doll was named after a member of the child's immediate family. The turtle and scissors were left within reach. Plastiline was given to the children. It is important to bear in mind that Pilagá children model well and have a fine sense of form. The boys, however, are inclined to be rougher than the girls in their handling of the material. That is to say, the sculpture of the boys is technically more like that of Jacob Epstein, the girls' sculpture more like that of Malvina Hoffman. Since the children have such a fine sense of form, failure to model an organ well is to be interpreted in most cases as a block.

In the first experiments some of the children put genitalia on the dolls to differentiate the sex. This was then made part of the experimental procedure. If breasts were not made and placed on the mother this was suggested. If a child seemed inhibited in using the material the examiner suggested that the baby doll be put to nurse. From that point on there was little activity on the part of the examiner, who usually pretended to be busy writing. When a child terminated his play the genitalia and breasts were not removed from the dolls by the examiner. It often happened, therefore, that at a subsequent experiment another child received the dolls with the organs already in position. If the dolls were not of the proper sex the child changed the sex spontaneously or the examiner suggested it.

Pilagá girls play with dolls of bone and of baked clay. Their mothers usually make the dolls for them. The clay dolls are females and the bone are males. The female dolls are about six inches long, have large, exposed breasts, and are frequently represented in a pregnant condition and with young at their breasts. The male dolls, on the other hand, are only about an inch long, and are simply bird bones wrapped in colored thread or cloth. Neither male nor female dolls have genitals.

Since boys do not play with dolls, this monograph contains more material on girls than it does on boys.

An important difference is to be noted between the way in which the girls play with their own dolls and the way they play with our dolls. When they play with their own dolls they do not name them. The dolls are called, rather, "the mother," "the father," "the child," "the widow," "the medicine man," etc. These dolls are then made to go through all the formal cultural patterns in an utterly impersonal way. The dolls go to look for food and distribute it to their relatives; the widow doll goes into isolation for the death of the husband and, as the doll mourns, the little girl sings the mourning song. The family goes to sleep, the children are arranged for the night, etc. Everything is subdued and depersonalized. In its impersonality this is very much like the operation of Pilagá social structure.

When playing with our dolls, on the other hand, the dolls were named after the members of the children's families, and the children treated the dolls quite differently. The play became intensely personal and hostilities were vividly acted out. Sexuality, completely absent when the girls played with their own dolls, was a characteristic feature of the play with ours.

It is interesting to note that when, as in the beginning of our work with the Pilagá children, our dolls were presented to them *unnamed*, the children merely went through the same type of play as with their own dolls. It must be concluded, therefore, that the *naming* of the dolls was a strong factor in setting off the whole train of personal reactions to be described in detail.

The presence of clay genitals on the dolls in the experiments is in keeping with the behavior of Pilagá children. Young children are permitted absolute sexual freedom. The adult sexual act is performed at night but without any attempt at concealment. Up to the age of five boys masturbate and practice pederasty unashamedly in broad daylight. The girls masturbate against one another in public, and at five years they start taking little boys to bed with them and attempting coitus. Open masturbation by rubbing against other children, games of snatching at genitalia, and open "coitus bees" in which groups of little boys and girls attempt coitus at night, continue until about the age of twelve. Children and adults joke constantly about sex, and sexual insults by children are common. Because of this situation a great deal of sexual material appears in the experiments.

In the protocols we have numbered in parentheses each hostile move; and we have numbered in italics each move that can be clearly interpreted as an attempt to put two or more figures in copulating position.

A defect in our work is the absence of the question "Why did you do that?" The question was not asked for fear of interfering with the flow of the activity, but the failure of the examiner to ask the question places the interpretation of the attacks on the "self" doll in doubt. In a few cases, after an attack on the self, the question was asked and noncommittal answers were received.

There are 24 cases: 13 females and 11 males. Some of the children played with the dolls only once, others played more often. Each session with the dolls is referred to as a 'trial.' One child has as many as twelve trials, but there is no rule as to the number of trials each child should have. The children were simply permitted to play when they wished.

The subjects range in age from 15 months to 12 years[2] and include children with a variety of behavior difficulties. One child is deaf and dumb.[3] Thus the material offers a wide range of conditions for study. It demonstrates that play of this kind can be used with success in the investigation of problems in infants and even in deaf mutes.

The larger part of this monograph is occupied with the problem of hostility. Nevertheless a considerable amount of material on sexuality and other factors related to child development was also brought out in the experiments. These data are discussed in separate sections.

[2] These ages are approximations based on the ethnologists' impressions. The Pilagá have no way of reckoning years.

[3] Discussed in Henry (6).

EXPERIMENTAL ANALYSIS OF HOSTILITY

Comparison between field observation and experimental results. It will be seen from Table II that the experimental results follow in general the field observations. With the exception of two cases there is a congruence between field and experimental results. The table shows that the greater

TABLE II
NUMBER OF HOSTILE MOVES IN ALL TRIALS

Name	No. of Trials	Mother	Father	Older 21-24 mos.	Older 25-36 mos.	Older 37-48 mos.	Older 49-60 mos.	Older 5 years or more	Younger 21-24 mos.	Younger 25-36 mos.	Younger 37-48 mos.	Younger 49-60 mos.	Younger 5 years or more	Self
1. Chaupá	2	4	2							1			5	3
2. Kar..í	1													
3. ———	5	6	6					10*–8		5				9
4. ——ní	9	12	4								5*		7	17
5. ——rodaikolík	12	6				19*				4				12
6. Deniki	7	6			1			13						3
7. Ñakéte	1													
8. Mátakana	4	3	1					0	10*					
9. Kayolí	6	24	19					0				15*		31
10. Kapíetn	1													
11. Simíti	8		3											
12. Dañakána	7	7	5			13								7
13. Anetolí	3	2	3					0					1	
14. Yatákana	4		1					0		1				
15. Maralú	1	1	4											
16. Wetél	4	5	1					9*						2
17. Katinorodí														
18. Kuwasiñítn	1													
19. Naichó	5													
20. Sorói	6	15	19		6									6
21. Lawésakachiyi	4		2											
22. Tanorowí	2													
23. Nakínak	1													
24. Koitaháa	2	2	2							2*				
Totals	96	93†	72		7	32		40	10	13	5	15	13	90

* Indicates intense hostility.

† 4, 5 and 6 have no father, and for that reason there was no father doll in most of their trials. The inclusion of a father doll would probably have made the totals for mother and father equal.

the overt hostility between siblings, the greater the number of attacks in the experiments. Thus, Darotoyí has three siblings: a baby sister, Simkoolí, three years his junior; a brother, Kanaidí, five and a half years his senior; and a sister, Chaupá, eight years his senior. Kanaidí makes Darotoyí's life miserable by constant torment—by beating, scolding, cursing, by sending home. The hostility between these two looms large in the field notes, whereas Darotoyí's hostility to his other siblings occupies a smaller place. The amount of hostility he displays toward these siblings in his experiments matches the observed behavior, for he makes the greatest number of hostile moves against Kanaidí.

The experimental results obtained with Yorodaikolík and Denikí are also congruent with field observation. Both in everyday life and in the doll-play these children show greater hostility toward Tapáñi, their sister, than they do toward each other.

Kayolí tortures and torments Kapíetn in everyday life and in the doll play she singles him out from her older sister for hostile attacks.

The play of Tapáñi and Chaupá, however, does not conform to observed behavior, for although in everyday life they show less hostility toward their infant siblings than to the next of age, in the doll play both of them show a higher total number of hostile acts directed toward the infant sibling than toward the next older. This contradiction is due to the strong social pressure against hurting infants. It reduces the overt hostility but exerts somewhat less control in the experimental situation.

The explanation of this greater hostility toward the infant is possibly to be sought in the fact that to both Chaupá and Tapáñi their infant siblings were a nuisance. They had to take care of them constantly, and many, many times could not play with the other children because of it. Were they to put their infant siblings down, they could expect a temper tantrum or at least a scream, accompanied at once by shouts from the adults and children: *adanokolík* or *adanolí*, [Take care of] your younger brother (or sister). The needs of the infant are a channel through which the intense repressed hostility of the Pilagá constantly expresses itself. The child's needs serve as an excuse for screaming angrily at the older sibling. Thus hostility is released by neighbors and relatives against the older sibling through the infant who, besides being a nuisance, becomes an electric point for the discharge of the hostility of others.

Comparison between sibling rivalry patterns in our culture and among the Pilagá. Levy has pointed out that in his own sibling rivalry esperiments: 1) there is a high percentage of "repetition of the pattern"[4] of hostility; 2) the "order" of attack "is determined by psychic events in the child's life";[5] 3) "either restitution or self-punishment follows the attacks as a direct and necessary sequel of the hostile behavior."[6]

[4] That is to say, each child follows a definite pattern of activity peculiar to it. Op. cit., pp. 28, 29.
[5] Ibid.
[6] Ibid., p. 29.

TABLE III*

DIRECTION: ORDER OF ATTACK

Name	I	II	III	IV	V	VI	VII	VIII	IX	X	XI	XII
Chaupá		S Ba B S M M Ba Ba M S										
Kanaidí	F											
Darotoyí	Ba M Ba M F B	F B F			M Ba B B S F B B Si Si S B S S S M B S Si B Si S Ba F Si Si S M Ba Ba M F Si Si B							
Tapáñi	M B & Ba M B & Ba		M B Ba	M F	All F S M B S M S All		S M M S M S S M Ba M B S Ba M S S					
Yorodaikolík			Si M	Si M S Ba M S Si		Si S	F Si	Si S Si S			Si S Si	Si M S Ba Ba M Si
Deniki		Si	Si	Si S M Si Si		Si M M B Si S	Si S Si M					
Ñakéte												
Mátakana	Ba	Ba F	Ba M Ba	Ba								
Kayolí		F M		272 moves. See protocol		F S B in law M Ba						
Kapíetn												
Simíti	F		F				F					
Dañakána	Si S	F	Si S M All	S Si Si S F Si M S Si M M S M F S Si F M M F S	Si							

TABLE III (*continued*)

Name	I	II	III	IV	V	VI	VII	VIII	IX	X	XI	XII
Anetolí	F		S M M M Si F									
Yatákana	M F	Ba	Si M	Si M F								
Maralú	M F F											
Wetél	F M M B B M S S M B B M	B										
Katinorodí												
Kuwasiñítn												
Naichó												
Sorói			M F	F F M M F B S F M M	F B M B B F S F F M M F S S M S B S F M S							
Lawésakachiyi				F								
Tanorowí												
Nakínak												
Koitaháa	F	Ba F M M Ba										

* Symbols used are: S, self; B, brother; Ba, baby; Si, sister; F, father; M, mother. Read downward, completing one column of symbols before going to the next.

It will be seen from Table III that Pilagá children rarely repeat the pattern of their hostility in the various trials. We suggest that this is due in part to the larger number of dolls in our experiments, that is, since the number of elements is increased, the number of possible combinations is also increased. Although this in no way affects the validity of Levy's results, it places a mechanical obstacle in the way of their verification in our own work. Since, also, our experiments did not limit the problem for the children, a great deal of play was concerned with non-hostile activity, hence the number of trials in which hostile acts were performed was greatly reduced.

In view of these facts, however, it is all the more significant that

Yorodaikolík and Denikí almost always find it necessary to begin their hostile activity with an attack on the doll representing their sister; and that Mátakana always begins with an attack on the baby doll.

Considering the data already brought forward regarding guilt feelings among the Pilagá, it is to be expected that Levy's third proposition would not hold among the Pilagá as it does in our culture. Thus in Trial I Daratoyí shows a great deal of hostility toward various members of his family, but there is no attack on the self and no restitution. In Trial V there is also a free release of hostility but, although there are several attacks on the self doll, there is no restitution.

It is interesting to examine the constellations in which the attacks on the self appear in Darotoyí's trials: 1) Kanaidí *self* Kanaidí; 2) Chaupá *self self* Kanaidí; Chaupá *self* baby; 3) Kanaidí *self* mother *self* Kanaidí. In the majority of cases where he attacks the baby—who is most closely hedged round with cultural sanctions—there is no attack on the self. It becomes difficult, therefore, to interpret the significance of the attacks on the self doll. In all children many of the attacks on the self may be due to "spread" of hostility.[7]

In Tapáñi's case it is interesting that the single restitutive act that does not apply to the self doll occurs in a very mild context. Her attacks on the self do not occur until Trial V where there is a general increase of activity. The attack on the self doll in Trial VII is concentrated and apparently purposive, but Tapáñi's spontaneous verbalization and her response to questions leaves the whole problem of motive unsolved. When in answer to the examiner's question: "Why does it bite you?" Tapáñi says: "Because it doesn't like me," she may simply be parroting the standardized idea about the turtle. The reply could be used to cloak the truth just as well as to reveal it.

The patterns of attack on the self in Yorodaikolík's trials are as follows: Trial IV: Tapáñi *self* mother; Tapáñi mother baby *self*; Trial VI: Tapáñi *self*; Trial VIII: Tapáñi *self*; Trial XII: Tapáñi *self* baby. In Trials VI and VIII we cannot, for the general reasons already given, interpret the attacks on the self as expressive of guilt. In addition, the special village and family attitudes toward Tapáñi make it unlikely that Yorodaikolík should feel remorse after attacking her. Not only is our whole history of the relationship between these siblings completely lacking in any manifestations of remorse, but Tapáñi is the village scapegoat. She is a child

---

[7] See Levy, op. cit., p. 53. Levy apparently has in mind here some sort of perseveration, whereby an action supported by a strong stimulus tends to repeat itself and even extend to objects other than the original one. Perhaps Holt's term *adience* would apply more precisely here.

upon whom the hostility of everyone—children and adults alike—openly concentrated. Tapáñi is "bad"; she is "stingy"; she is "ugly"; she is "undersized"; she is an "old lady." With the exception of the last, poor Tapáñi is all of these. Hence the accusations are just. As a matter of fact, Tapáñi would be treated much worse in our culture than she is among the Pilagá. She is a bully and a glutton and uses her bullying to satisfy her gluttony. It is hard to believe that Yorodaikolík should have felt remorse after attacking the Tapáñi doll—especially when we consider that her own mother detested her and at times even stimulated her younger children to attack Tapáñi.

In Trial VIII, in answer to the question: "Why are you bitten?" Yorodaikolík says: "Because I am sick." This may mean: (a) "Because I am a general nuisance"; or (b) "Because I am weak and cannot defend myself." On the other hand the answer may be very remote from the subject. In Trial XII it is doubtful that the squashing of the penis represents an attack on the self in any realistic sense. What Yorodaikolík does is change the penis to a vagina. He then improves the vagina of the mother doll, puts breasts on the baby doll, and then puts a clitoris in the vagina of the Tapáñi doll. Thus the changing of the penis on the self doll to a vagina is but one in a series of movements concerned with female organs.[8]

In Trial XII Yorodaikolík, after drowning the baby doll, says: "Denikí drowned. I, on the other hand, *did not drown,*" thereby reassuring himself that he had not been punished.

In Trial IV the attacks on the self come as a prelude to an attack on the mother doll—a comparatively rare sequence in the Pilagá experiments—and as a sequel to getting all the other dolls out of the way. In the Pilagá experiments one often gets the impression that the direction of the turtle against the self represents the actualization of a generalized anxiety. This type of activity has its precise analogues in everyday life. One of the commonest is the dog-bite game. In this game the children provoke a puppy or a fairly harmless older dog to attack them. Then they run off, but return again and again. This game is played in a state of high excitement and is accompanied by wild laughter. No one is ever hurt. Another game of this type is the iron wheel game, a game that takes various forms. The commonest is that in which a child impersonates a jaguar or a lunatic and chases all the other children with the iron wheel which he pushes before him on the end of a stick. This game is also characterized by great excitement and laughter. The children are careful not to hurt one another. In

---

[8] For discussion of sexual activity see section on Sexuality.

both these games the thrill lies in the escape from the threat. An added attraction is that for a few moments, but repeatedly during the play, the fleeing child becomes the center of attention of the other children—and even of the dog.

Yorodaikolík's restoring acts are peculiar in character—that is, peculiar to the Pilagá—for unlike similar movements in the Levy experiments they do not appear to come as "*direct and necessary sequels* of the hostile behavior."[9] In Trial VI the restitution of the baby doll comes after a long series of vicious attacks on the *sister* doll and on the *self* doll. It is also important to note that Yorodaikolík's release of hostility was interrupted by Mátakana, who took the knife away. It appears, indeed, as if the interruption had started a whole new system of activities—a system, however, which began in the same way as the trial itself began. Thus, the trial began with the baby and mother made to copulate; and after being deprived of the knife Yorodaikolík again put the baby and mother dolls in copulating position.

In Trial XII there is again no indication that placing the baby doll beside the mother doll is a "necessary sequel" to hostility, for there has been no hostile act. In this case the restoration of the baby doll appears as a single move in the development of play *which has no plot*.

In the analytical summary of Yorodaikolík's trials we have listed "makes shoes for mother doll" and "makes hat (brim)" also as restitutive acts. We have done this in an effort to present in the analysis all possible relevant material rather than because these acts seem to us to be truly acts of restoration. It is true that putting shoes on the mother doll might be the psychic sequel to jabbing an object into her foot; but the "hat" on the sister doll hardly seems to be a restitution for blinding. In addition, it is to be noted that both of these acts come after many intervening minutes of unrelated activity.

In Denikí Trials IV and VII, his self-directed attacks come before and after attacks on the sister doll; in his Trial VI the attack on the self precedes an attack on the mother. It is difficult to interpret these self-directed moves because of the almost complete absence of verbalization. Nevertheless it is important to note that what is true of Yorodaikolík's attitude toward Tapáñi (the sister) is very likely true of Denikí's. There are no restitutive acts.

Mátakana always begins her hostile activity on the baby doll—almost exclusively the object of her hostility. She expresses her hostility but in an extremely mild way, and there are no attacks on the self. Acts listed as restitutive occur in Trial II where, after trying to make the baby go back where it came from, she puts it to nurse; and where, after sexual activity with the father and baby dolls and manipulation of the self and sister dolls, she gives the baby back to the mother; in Trial III where she asks the examiner to replace the arm of the father doll; and again inTrial III where, after sexual activity with the father doll and a derogatory remark about the baby doll, it is restored to the mother and the play terminates.

Mátakana's play is characterized by considerable verbalization, but in only one act of "restoration" does she give any indication of the meaning that type of activity has for her. As she places the baby doll beside the mother doll in Trial III she says: "At last her vagina is finished," i.e., at last the mother has been delivered, and hence the baby is a fact. He is born, and his natural place is beside the mother.

The most obvious and clear-cut acts of restitution were performed by Dañakána—one of the least violent of the children in the village. Dañakána is perfectly able to hold her own in any quarrel, but she does not get herself into fights the way so many of the other children do; she hardly ever begs, and she could scarcely be called greedy. Her antagonism toward her sister Simíti, who is four years her senior, emerges, however, in the experiments. In Trial VII, for example, she puts the sister doll on the ground and says, apparently quite innocently, "She's diving." But when JH comes in Dañakána swiftly seizes the doll and puts it back in her hand with the self doll. This sudden gesture of "restitution" indicates the strong hostility and anxiety connected with the apparently harmless: "She's diving." Diving, of course, is one step removed from drowning.

Many of Dañakána's superficially innocent movements with the sister doll appear to be charged with hostile intent. Thus, earlier in the same trial she replaces the sister doll on the play box as soon as the sister appears at the door. The hostility and restoration are clearer in Trial III where, after attacking the sister doll with the turtle, she remarks by way of restitution: "My sister's cute little breasts." Still earlier in Trial III her appreciative: "Look at Simíti's water pot," anticipates the contemplated attack with the turtle.

Thus, in at least two cases Dañakána's restitutive acts appear under the influence of extremely wary, almost completely concealed hostility. The only things that reveal the activity as charged with hostility and anxiety are her sudden movements stimulated by interruptions.

In Yatákana's play each trial begins with removal of the breasts either from the mother or the sister doll. In all the trials she restores the breasts almost at once; thus giving the impression of a desire to remove the clay as a "stuck-on" object[10] rather than an act of restitution.

Thus, in general, in the Pilagá experiments the restitutive acts and the movements against the self do not occur where they would be expected in terms of similar behavior in children in our own culture. The movements against the self doll do not appear to be acts of self-punishment because they do not occur where hostile acts would socially be most strongly disapproved. For similar reasons the acts of "restitution" do not seem to be associated with the harm done, but appear rather as incidents in generalized, plotless, play. On the whole the problem of the movements against the self doll has not been satisfactorily solved. Suggested reasons for these movements are: 1) *spread* of hostility; 2) "balancing of accounts," that is, the child may feel in less danger of retaliation if he does to himself what he has done to the other dolls; 3) actualization of anxiety; 4) self-regard.[11]

Comparison between the Levy procedure and that used among the Pilagá. Levy's procedure was therapeutic and designed to facilitate the release of hostility. The experimental situation was set up as a dramatic performance in which the child was given the leading role by the examiner. Levy shaped the play situation as follows:[12]

"The patient is told that we are to play a game. For the game we need a mother, a baby and an older a sister (or brother). We use the amputation doll to represent the mother, a celluloid baby doll, and a larger doll for the older sister (or brother). The examiner says, 'The mother must feed the baby.' He then points to the chest of the amputation doll and says, 'But she has no breasts. Let's make some.' The examiner makes one breast, the child makes the other. . . . After the breasts are placed in position on the mother doll, the baby doll is put in the nursing position, the mother's arms encircling it. The child is asked to name the baby and the sister (or brother).

"The examiner then says, 'Now this is the game. The sister comes and sees a new baby at the mother's breast. She (or he) sees it for the first time. Now what does she (or he) do? Do whatever you think.' The child is encouraged with such phrases as 'Go ahead,' 'Don't be afraid.' The experiment may be repeated several times.

"After the 'controlled' situation has been utilized in this way, the examiner may then stimulate activity in various ways. These methods of releasing the

---

[10] Levy remarks that "children tend to remove any stuck-on object" no matter where it is placed, and often with no hostile intent. Op. cit., p. 31.

[11] See section on Self-regard.

[12] Op. cit., p. 9.

rivalry are described in the individual cases. They consist largely in using such phrases as, 'When the sister (or brother) saw the baby she thought, 'The nerve, at my mother's breast!' Or the child is told, 'That's really your baby brother and this doll is you'."

The patients' movements were interpreted in terms of the dramatic situation and the problem ("What does she (or he) do?").[13] For example, the child's touching the dolls was interpreted as inhibited hostility; and playing with materials outside the play set-up was considered an escape from the situation.

In the Pilagá experiments, however, no situation was presented to the children. Were we to graph our experiments as Levy has graphed[14] his, vectors such as "escape," "undirected hostility," and "attack shunted to other objects" would therefore be missing. Play with our dolls was "free play." Since no stimulus was directly presented we could not interpret a child's cutting its own skirt as "attack shunted to other objects." The vector "inactivity" that appears so often in Levy's graphs would be omitted in graphs of the Pilagá experiments because the absence of any strong simulus to activity seemed to rob inactivity of any significance accessible to us.

A word is necessary regarding Levy's principle of "interpretation . . . based on the sequence of events."[15] He explains this as follows: " . . . the interpretation of any item is based on the sequence of events. When, in any particular case, a gap occurs in a sequence which in other cases is completed, the meaning is implied. The basis of interpretation is then inferential, as though to say, if the sequence had gone on uninterrupted it would have taken the form observed in the behavior of those children who had frequently completed such a sequence. The assumption is the same in the case of a child who repeats three out of four acts in a logical sequence in the first, second or third trial, completing the chain in the fourth trial. Since the objectives in a given line of activity are clearly revealed, it is easy to infer how events would proceed. . . . " It is clear, however, that it was the experimental situation set up by Levy that was fundamental in making possible this type of interpretation. One can understand the child's being constantly unconsciously urged on by the question: "Now what does he (or she) do?" when he or she sees the new

[13] Op. cit., pp. 26–27.

[14] Levy has divided the patients' behavior in the play situation into seven types: I. Inactivity. II. Escape (out of the room). III. Escape (into distraction). IV. Inhibited movements. V. Attack from a distance. VI. Undirected hostility. VII. Attack shunted to other objects. Each of these forms of behavior is represented by a special type of vector in his graphs. See op. cit., pp. 26 and 39–51.

[15] Op. cit., pp. 26–27.

sibling at the mother's breast. The situation is compelling and demands a solution. Since in our experiments the question is missing, nothing demands an answer, and a movement toward the dolls might mean anything.

The reader will notice that in our experiments there is an entire absence of attack on the breasts. Since it is no exaggeration to say that breasts are and remain crucial in the life of the Pilagá—the adults remember the "delicious taste" of their mothers' milk—and since the deprivation of the breast has effects in the life of the Pilagá that make breast deprivation in our culture seem a mere April shower, one naturally wonders why there is an almost total absence of attack on the breasts in our experiments. Similarly one wonders why, since weaning is so early in our culture, and bottle feeding so common, Levy's experiments show so many attacks on the breasts.

When further comparisons are made between nursing experiences in our culture and early nursing experience among the Pilagá, the contrast in attitudes toward the breasts in Levy's experiments and ours must seem even more striking. Among the Pilagá the entire naked body of the infant is pressed against its mother's naked body. While it sucks at one breast it manipulates the other with one hand. The Pilagá child is nursed many times a day. When the child is being carried on a sling against its mother's body the child treats the breast almost like an "all-day sucker." In our culture, on the other hand, nursing is by the clock and the period is fixed. Only the child's oral region is in contact with its mother's flesh, and the other breast is inaccessible to his hands. Thus there is a great difference in the importance of the breasts to the children of the two cultures. How, then, shall we explain the absence of attack on the breasts in the Pilagá experiments? It seems very likely that much of the difference in results rests on a difference in experimental techniques of the investigators.

Levy's procedure tends to focus attention on the breasts: "The mother must feed the baby. . . . But she has no breasts." "The sister comes and sees a new baby at the mother's breast. She (or he) sees it for the first time. Now what does she (or he) do?" In later trials Levy's stimulus sentence is: "When the sister (or brother) saw the baby she (or he) thought, 'the nerve, at my mother's breast'!" The presentation of the situation in this way would tend to draw the breasts in particular into the child's sphere of hostile interest.

In the Pilagá experiments there were no factors which would tend to give the breasts particular importance. The child was left mostly to its own devices. The making of breasts by the child was generally spontaneous, and if the child did not make breasts the examiner pointed out the absence of breasts simply as a feature that made the mother's body incomplete. There was no concentration on breasts to the exclusion of other anatomical features and no dramatic situation was especially set up in which breasts were given a prominent role.

Form and frequency of hostile moves. Levy's table of *Forms of Hostility to Breasts*[16] gives 13 forms. He points out[17] that "the removal of the breasts is regarded as a hostile manifestation since it is followed in every case but one by some form of hostility—pinching, crushing with fingers, stamping with feet, tearing apart, etc. In the one case in which removal alone occurs, the meaning is hostile, as shown by the play of events." It is interesting to examine the Pilagá cases of removal of breasts in the light of Levy's observations. Denikí, Trial VII (5),[18] cuts the breasts into small pieces with scissors, but Anetolí, Trial III (4) and (5), uses the same clay to fashion organs for the father and mother dolls. Yatákana, Trial II uses the same clay to make a better pair of breasts; in Trial III after removing all the clay parts from the mother and sister dolls she uses it to remake the breasts; in Trial IV (1) she again uses the clay to replace the breasts. Sorói, Trial III (1) tries to put the breasts on a smaller doll—("stealing" (?)). Denikí and Soroí, therefore, appear to be the only children whose behavior with the breasts might be said to match the behavior of Levy's subjects. The *total number of removals* by Pilagá children was 8; in Levy's subjects the total number of *forms*[19] of hostility to the breasts was 49.[20] Hence, both in number and variety the difference between our results and Levy's is very great.

A comparison of our tables of forms of hostility with Levy's shows great differences. Levy's table of *Forms of Hostility to Baby* shows 34 forms, of which 25 are active and 9 are verbal. Our table shows only 15 forms, of which 7 are active and 8 are verbal, although there are 59 Pilagá trials for children with younger siblings, while Levy has 45. It could hardly be

[16] Op. cit., p. 34.

[17] Ibid., p. 31.

[18] Numbers in brackets indicate the number of the "hostile" moves in the trial.

[19] The number of hostile *acts* is to be distinguished from the number of *forms* of hostility in that the number of acts refers to the mere sum of all the hostile moves whereas the number of forms refers to the number of different *types* of act. Thus, if a child cuts the dolls 3 times, blinds them twice, and insults them 5 times, he has made 10 hostile acts but only 3 types or forms of act.

[20] Removal and cutting of the breasts by Pilagá children were the only forms of activity with breasts that might be interpreted as hostile. Hence there were *two* forms of (hostile?) activity by Pilagá children as against 49 by Levy's subjects. The gross number of hostile *acts* by Levy's subjects is much higher than 49.

Name	Chaupá	Kanaidí	Darotoyí	Tapáti	Yorodaikolík	Deniki	Ñagéte	Mátakana	Kayolí	Kapletn	Simíti	Dañakána	Anetolí	Yatákana	Maralí	Wetél	Katinorodí	Kuwasiñítn	Naicbó	Sorói	Lawésakachiyí	Tanorowí	Nakínak	Koítaháa
No. of Trials	1	1	5	9	12	7	1	4	6	1	8	7	3	4	1	4	0	1	5	5	4	2	1	2
Age	12	9	4	8	4	1	9	3	8	3	10	6	9	5	12	6	10	6	6	7	6	10	6	3
Sex	f	m	m	f	m	m	f	f	f	m	f	f	f	f	m	m	m	m	f	f	m	f	m	m

ACTIVITY

Mild Attack
Removal
Disposal
Intercourse
Uses against other doll
Transfer of hostility to
 examiner
Turtle bites
Change of sex
Drops
Puts object on head
Pushes on ground

Simple assault
Shakes fist
Throwing
Knocks down
Banging
Sticking
Turtle bites
Amputation
Cutting
Blinding
Swinging
Drowning
Castration
Run over

VERBAL
Change of identity
Insult
Removal
Disposal
Denial of identity
Weeping
Deserted
Falling
Bitten
Change of sex
Hitting
Deflowered
Amputation
Blinding
Crippled
Burning
Drowning
Castration
Death
Killing

* This table contains all the forms of hostility that occur in the doll play. The order of the listing of the forms adheres as closely as possible to the order of the separate tables. The forms are listed in order of their intensity within each group. Thus, in "mild attack" the severest form of hostility is "pushes on the ground," whereas in "verbal" the severest form is "killing."

TABLE IV

FORMS OF HOSTILITY TO BABY*

Name	Chaupá	Kanaidí	Darotoyí	Tapáti	Yorodaitolík	Deniki	Ñakéte	Mátakana	Kayolí	Kapíetn	Simíti	Dañakína	Anetolí	Yatákana	Maralí	Wetél	Katinorodí	Kuwasiñáitn	Naichó	Sorói	Lawésakachíyi	Tanorowí	Nakinak	Kóitaháa
No. of Trials	1	1	5	9	12	7	1	4	6	1	8	7	3	4	1	4	0	1	5	5	4	2	1	2
Age	12	9	4	8	4	1	9	3	8	3	10	6	9	5	12	6	10	6	6	7	6	10	6	3
Sex	f	m	m	f	m	m	f	f	f	m	f	f	f	f	m	m	m	m	f	f	m	f	m	m
ACTIVITY																								
Mild Attack																								
Removal			3					23																2
Disposal				4				24							2									
Intercourse								1																
Turtle bites†	1		15	157					4															
Simple Assault																								
Throws down													3											
Turtle bites			15																					
Drowning						12‡																		
Castration						12‡																		
VERBAL																								
Insult								23																
Removal																								
Disposal				4				24																
Weeping																								2
Falling																								2
Bitten			15		1																			
Amputation									6															
Drowning						12‡																		

* Each digit stands for the number of the trial except where otherwise noted.

† I.e., turtle is made to strike against a doll. See Chapter III, p. 30. For explanation of why "turtle bites" appears on both categories, cf. p. 53.

‡ Trial XII.

said that this difference is due to lack of imagination in Pilagá children, for in the number of forms of hostility to the mother the Pilagá and the American children are equal. The restraint in the treatment of the baby doll seems to be due to four factors. 1) The cultural pressure against attack on the baby; 2) the small amount of reciprocal hostility; 3) lack of dramatic focus in the procedure; 4) the free spreading of hostility to other members of the family in the experiments. The last factor is particularly important, for it will be seen from Table II that the *gross number* of hostile moves against the parents is greater than that against all of the siblings put together. In addition, it will be seen that attacks on *older* siblings account for more than half of the total number of hostile moves against siblings. The absence of limiting factors in the experiment has permitted the hostility to spread to the family in general.

TABLE V

FORMS OF HOSTILITY TO SIBLINGS

Name	Chaupá	Kanaidí	Darotoyí	Tapáñi	Yorodaikolík	Denikí	Ñakéte	Mátakana	Kayolí	Kapletn	Simíti	Dañakána	Anetolí	Yatákana	Maralí	Wetél	Katinorodí	Kuwasíñitn	Naichó	Soróí	Lawésakachiyí	Tanorowí	Nakínak	Koitaháa
No. of Trials	1	1	5	9	12	7	1	4	6	1	8	7	3	4	1	4	0	1	5	5	4	2	1	2
Age	12	9	4	8	4	1	9	3	8	3	10	6	9	5	12	6	6	6	6	7	6	10	6	3
Sex	f	m	m	f	m	m	f	f	f	m	f	f	f	f	f	m	m	m	f	f	m	f	m	m
ACTIVITY																								
Mild Attack																								
Removal												5												
Disposal			2		47							13												
Turtle bites			15	157	8							134				1				45				
Simple Assault																								
Shakes fist at					3																			
Throwing				3		3																		
Throws down						2																		
Banging						4																		
Turtle bites			15																					
Amputation						67																		
Cutting					6	467																		
Blinding					12*																			
Castration			1		6																			
VERBAL																								
Change of identity					7																			
Insult				1	12*												2							
Disposal			2		4							13												
Bitten			5		5							4												
Deflowered					4																			
Blinding					12*																			
Castration			1		6																			
Death					11*																			
Killing					6																			

* Trial XI and XII.

On comparing Tables IV and V with Table III it can be seen that the total number of attacks on the baby doll and the total number of forms of hostility to the baby doll are less than the total number of attacks on the sibling dolls and the total number of forms of hostility to the sibling dolls. This is due in part to the cultural pressure against injuring a baby sibling,[21] in part to the greater number of sibling dolls.

In Levy's work there are 34 forms of hostility to the baby and only 19

---

[21] Kayolí, Table II, shows 15 attacks on the baby doll. Since, however, 14 of them occurred during Trial IV when there was tremendous activity with the turtle, with apparently very little emotional charge, these 14 moves cannot be given the same weight as more highly charged activity in other trials.

TABLE VI

FORMS OF HOSTILITY TO MOTHER

Name	Chaupá	Kanaidí	Darotoyf	Tapáti	Yorodaikolík	Deniki	Ñakéte	Mátakana	Kayolí	Kapíetn	Simíti	Dañakána	Anetolí	Yatákana	Maralí	Wetél	Katinorodí	Kuwasiñítn	Naichó	Sorói	Lawésakachiyi	Tanorowí	Nakínak	Koitañáa
No. of Trials	1	1	5	9	12	7	1	4	6	1	8	7	3	4	1	4	0	1	5	5	4	2	1	2
Age	12	9	4	8	4	1	9	3	8	3	10	6	9	5	12	6	10	6	6	7	6	10	6	3
Sex	f	m	m	f	m	m	f	f	f	m	f	f	f	f	m	m	m	m	f	f	f	m	m	m
ACTIVITY																								
Mild Attack																								
Disposal					4								3											
Intercourse								3						4										
Transfer of hostility to examiner			3																					
Turtle bites	2		15	157	4				4				4				1			45				
Change of sex									5															
Drops																								2
Puts object on head					12*																			
Simple Assault																								
Shakes fist at				3																				
Knocks down					4																			2
Sticking					12*																			
Turtle bites			15																					
Amputation						6																		
Cutting						467			6															
Castration																				3				
Run over																1								
VERBAL																								
Change of identity				7																				
Insult								3					3			1								
Disposal				4																				
Denial of identity				7																				
Deserted								2																
Bitten			5	15																				
Hitting								2																

* Trial XII.

to the mother. Our tables show 15 forms of hostility to the baby and 21 forms of hostility to the mother. The therapeutic goal of Levy's experiments, however, seems to have had an effect on his results. In order to treat certain behavior problems in children, it was necessary that Levy not only give definite stimulus phrases, but that at times he also collaborate in the release of hostility. The dramatic focusing of attention on the baby and Levy's frequent and necessary verbal participation in the play facilitated the release of hostility to the baby doll, as he intended it should. The therapeutic value of this procedure is well known, but it is probable also that it would have had an effect on the differential release

TABLE VII
FORMS OF HOSTILITY TO FATHER

Name	Chaupá	Kanaidí	Darotoyí	Tapáti	Yorodakollk	Deniki	Ñakéte	Mátakana	Kayolí	Kapíetn	Simíti	Dañakána	Anetolí	Yatákana	Maralú	Wetél	Katinorodí	Kuwasiñítn	Naichó	Soróí	Lawésakachiyi	Tanorowí	Nakfnak	Koitañá
No. of Trials	1	1	5	9	12	7	1	4	6	1	8	7	3	4	1	4	0	1	5	5	4	2	1	2
Age	12	9	4	8	4	1	9	3	8	3	10	6	9	5	6	6	10	6	6	7	6	10	6	3
Sex	f	m	m	f	m	m	f	f	f	m	f	f	f	f	m	m	m	m	m	f	f	f	m	m
ACTIVITY																								
Mild Attack																								
Disposal								2			13													
Uses against other doll			4										3											
Turtle bites	1	15	5						4				4		1					45				
Pushes on ground								2					2											
Simple Assault																								
Turtle bites		15																						
Amputation									6		38			1						3				
Cutting													1											
Blinding				7																				
Swinging														1										
Castration													2								4	4		2
Run over														1										
VERBAL																								
Insult		2	4										7	1										1
Disposal		2																						
Bitten		15	5																					
Change of sex													2											
Hitting									2															
Amputation									6															
Crippled																					4			
Burning																								2
Castration													2	3										
Death		5																		3				

of hostility. The Pilagá children were left to themselves, and released hostility a little more against the parents than against the siblings (not including the baby). Actually, in eight cases the number of hostile moves against mother and father dolls was greater than against the sibling dolls, and in seven cases it was the reverse.

Since in the Pilagá experiments the examiner took no part in the direction or facilitation of hostility, and since the dolls represent all the members of the family, a rough quantitative estimate of what might be called the *hostility differential* seems possible. That is to say, we can attempt to determine how much hostility each child has toward his parents and how much toward his siblings as a group. Naturally, because of the varied manner of expression we cannot give this estimate in terms more precise than *greater* or *less*.

In order for us to show that the *number* of hostile moves is an index of the child's true feelings, e.g., if the total number of his hostile moves against the parents is greater than against the siblings, this number really indicates that his basic hostility is greater toward his parents than toward his siblings, we must show that the performance is *consistent*. Otherwise it is obvious that there must almost always be a difference between the two totals (parents vs. siblings) even if there be no fundamental difference in attitude toward parents or siblings. It will be seen from Table II, for example, that Darotoyí has a higher total of hostile moves against the siblings than against the parents, but examination of Table VIII shows that his performance is not consistent. Thus, in Trials I and II the hostility to the parents and siblings is about equal. It is only in Trial V that the attacks on the siblings are the more numerous. Hence we could not, on the basis of a mere count of his moves, conclude that he is more hostile to his siblings. Tapáñi makes more attacks on the parents than she does on the siblings, but the analysis given in Table VIII of the attacks in all her trials shows that they are almost equally divided among siblings and parents. That is to say, that the number of trials in which she made a greater number of hostile moves against the parents is almost equal to the number of trials in which she made a greater number of hostile moves against the siblings.

. If, however, the trend of the trials is always, or nearly always, in the same direction, i.e., if it does not veer from the parents to the siblings but shows a certain *consistent trend*, then we may conclude that *number* of hostile moves is a true index of the child's feelings. Table VIII includes all cases for which we have two or more trials. Before discussing the table it is necessary to point out that its validity is somewhat marred by the cultural sanction against attacks on infants.

Darotoyí and Tapáñi give rather inconsistent pictures. They veer in their play from attacks on the parents to attacks on the siblings. Yorodaikolík, however, shows a thoroughgoing consistency of attack on the siblings. So does his brother Denikí. So does Mátakana. Kayolí and Simíti are consistent in their attacks on the parents. An interesting case is that of Dañakána, for although the total number of her hostile moves against parents and sister is almost equal, the general trend is against the sister, and this in spite of the fact that there are two parent dolls but only one sister doll. Not so, however, for Sorói, for her attacks are consistently on the parents.

Thus seven out of fourteen cases give consistent pictures; two are inconsistent; one is marred, and six lack data. It appears, therefore, that in

TABLE VIII
CONSISTENCY OF HOSTILITY TREND*

Name	Number of hostile moves against mother and father. Trial												Number of hostile moves against all siblings. Trial												Number of trials predominantly hostile to parents	Number of trials predominantly hostile to siblings	Number of trials with equal hostility
	1	2	3	4	5	6	7	8	9	10	11	12	1	2	3	4	5	6	7	8	9	10	11	12			
Darotoyí	3	2											3	1											1	1	1
Tapáñi		2	1	4	7		4						4		2		19		3						3	2	1
Yorodaikolík			1	2	5	2	1					3			1	5	3		1				2	5	0	6	1
Deniki				1			3											4	2	4					1	4	0
Mátakana		1	1											1	3	3		7							0	4	0
Kayolí		2		66	1	4							1	5	3	15		1							4	0	0
Simíti	1		2					1								1									3	0	0
Dañakáña		1	4	10									3		5	7	1								2	3	0
Anetolí	1		4											1	1										2	0	0
Yatákana				1										1											1	1	0
Wetél	7												8												0	2	0
Soroí		3	10	21												1	5								3	0	0
Lawésakachiyi	1																								1	0	0
Koitañá		3		2										2											2	0	0

* The numbers under each trial represent the number of hostile moves in each trial. The columns on the left represent the total number of moves against the father *and* the mother; the columns on the right represent the total number of hostile moves against *all* siblings.

seven cases *the hostility operates constantly in one direction with more force than in another.*[22]

We have divided the hostile acts into three classes, following rather closely Levy's categories of "mild attack," "simple assault," and "verbal."[23] These provide reasonably objective criteria and seem, therefore, satisfactory for our purposes. It will be seen from the tables that our experiments show none of the "primitive hostile forms" (Levy's third category) so common in Levy's work.[24] This absence may be ascribed in part to the children's respect for the property of others, and in part to the absence of activation. We should take account, however, of the fact that the mild forms of attack far outnumber in frequency even the s.a. (simple assault) forms. This raises an important problem. In view of the reasons given above we can understand why there should be no primitive forms of hostility, but why should there be so few s.a. forms? Is it because the turtle made release easy? An analysis of the performance of individual children may throw some light on the problem. In Table V it will be seen that the nine s.a. forms were contributed by only four children[25]—an astonishing fact, especially when we consider that three of these children are siblings. Of these four children three were able to use the turtle; the fourth, a baby, could not. It will be noted that activity with the turtle has usually been classed as mild hostility. This has been done because movements with the turtle were so numerous and appeared accompanied by little affect. The turtle could, however, be used as an instrument of simple assault, and whenever it was made to bite ferociously, and the activity was accompanied by obvious exultation, such activity was classified as simple assault. Much of Darotoyí's activity with the turtle belongs in this category. Thus it cannot be urged that the turtle alone was responsible for the generally low frequency of simple assault forms. Furthermore, some of the children to whom the turtle was accessible abandoned it in favor of more satisfactory forms of release. A wider survey of the simple assault forms to the siblings, baby, and mother reveals the striking

[22] This problem should be studied in a more "clinical" situation where outside influences would not upset the procedure.

[23] Naturally the forms of hostility are different in the Pilagá experiments from what they are in Levy's. The differences are due to both experimental procedure and culture. The full list of the various forms of hostility encountered in the Pilagá experiments is given in the Master Table. For the forms found in Levy's experiments see op. cit., pp. 32, 33, and 38.

[24] Levy includes in this category the severest forms of hostility: crushing, tearing apart, biting, etc.

[25] If Tapáñi were not counted, the number of forms of hostility would be the same, and we would have 3 instead of 4 children.

fact that Darotoyí, Yorodaikolík, and Denikí—all boys—account for 84 per cent of the simple assault acts. This naturally suggests that boys are more violent than girls; or that attitudes of boys toward their families are more hostile than those of girls; or that boys are less repressed than girls. Quantitative statements, however, need quantitative evidence and we do not have enough data to make any general statement in this regard. It is possible, nevertheless, to say that among Pilagá children *males and females resemble each other in regard to the amount of violent activity they manifest.*

The distribution of the simple assault forms to the father is more uniform. In spite of the concentration of simple assault forms in these three children it will be noted that even in their play the mild forms exceed in number the simple assault forms. In all but two of Levy's cases, however, (Cases 3 and 11) the severer forms of hostility exceed in frequency the milder forms.

Inhibition of hostility. Commenting on our work Levy remarks[26] that "the play of hostility does not mount, as in [Levy's] S-R experiments. They would keep well within the classification of mild to moderate display of hostility, chiefly mild." He suggests that this may be due to absence of stimulation or to inhibition of hostile movements. Another possibility is, of course, that Pilagá children are simply "not so hostile." It is a difficult problem, and in the absence of techniques for measuring such attitudes as are here discussed, it seems to us best to leave the question open. On the other hand it seems pertinent to discuss the factors that operate in the inhibition of hostile acts, and to ask: Why do Pilagá children inhibit their hostility at all; and what are the circumstances that assist this inhibition?

In another part of this monograph we pointed out that corporal sanctions and insults were the characteristic justice of the child world, where the law of an "eye for an eye and a tooth for a tooth" prevails. It was suggested also that it was the fear of retaliation rather than remorse which motivated the attacks on the self. It is very likely, therefore, that fear of retaliation is one of the factors that inhibits hostility[27] and hence keeps it well within the limits of the mild category with most of the children.

Perhaps in no other aspect of child life is the fear of retaliation more manifest than in the little girls' intervillage boxing bouts. In these bouts groups of embattled little girls fight each other with fists. Considering

---

[26] Levy (11).
[27] See also Levy (10), p. 72.

the anger of the children these bouts are remarkably mild. The girls face each other in two long lines and pound each other on the arms. It is a strikingly quiet give-and-take. But woe to the girl who strikes a blow that is the least bit too heavy, or which falls on the body or face instead of on the arms! She will be attacked ferociously by her opponent and driven from the fight. It is no wonder that in these fights children are rarely hurt. From time to time one child or another goes too far and is soundly whipped by her opponent; and there was the case of Chaupá who attacked her opponent with four inch thorns and had to escape to a relative's house to avoid a mob of infuriated little girls.

In addition to the fear of retaliation, which may be considered as a direct influence on the display of hostility, we must also take account of the sexual activity of the children as furnishing a diversion. Pilagá children pass hours each day in violent sexual games of a rather simple character. One of these is what we have called the genitalia-snatching game. In this game the children go hurtling after one another trying to touch each other's genital. Usually the boys chase the girls. Often they throw them down, and try to touch the girl's genital, while she shrieks with excitement. Sometimes the fall hurts and she cries. When the boys have caught one girl the other little girls dash up and beat off the boys. Then the boys chase the other little girls and the situation is repeated. The play may go on for hours, and it is accompanied by the excited screams of the children. This blending of violence and sexuality extends to many details of play. In the following scenes sexuality and violence are inextricably mixed.

Kapíetn fights with Yatákana, thrusts his hand against her vulva and says: "It stinks." Darotoyí says: "Look here, Zunia" and shows her the corn he is eating. Tapáñi and Yatákana box. When Yatákana turns toward ZH, Tapáñi pounds her on the back. Tapáñi separates Yorodaikolíks buttocks and drags him off the dirt pile. Yatákana snatches at Kapíetn's penis from behind. Then she pounds him on the back. All the boys including Denikí are around ZH. Yorodaikolík, Darotoyí, and Denikí are masturbating. Darotoyí has exposed his glans by pulling back the foreskin. Yorodaikolík shoves his foot against it and pushes him down.

Simíti pushes Nakínak hard and he falls down on his belly. Then she puts her hand on his testicles from behind.

While girls are playing their bouncing game[28] the boys go behind them and touch their genitals. Then they join the game. Then the children push one another over until Kayolí's nose starts to bleed.

---

[28] In this game the girls squat on their haunches and bounce up and down.

Kayolí, Ñakéte, Dañakána, and Sorói are playing the game of touching each other's genitals. They try to pull off Dañakána's skirt and she weeps.

The little girls Dañakána and Naichó, and the little boys Yorodaikolík and Darotoyí are playing the following game on a number of skins they have laid down for the purpose: the girls play their bouncing game and the boys try to imitate them. Then a girl falls down and boys jump on top of her and masturbate against her. Naichó lies down more often than Dañakána and for a longer time. As soon as the boys leap on Dañakána she gets up. Her role is mostly driving off the boys.

In the following scene the boys Waidolkáchigi,[29] Katinorodí, Maralú, Kovyoró,[30] Nakínak, Darotoyí, Wetél, Kuwasiñítn, and one other; and the girls Kayolí, Tanorowí, Chaupá, Simíti, Ñakéte, Dañakána, Sorói, Yatákana, and one girl[31] from another village, are engaged in activity centering around a coitus-bee. Waidolkáchigi is lying down with Simíti, and Kovyoró with Tanorowí. The little girls ask JH and Suvyaraikítn to ask the little boys to come as their sleeping partners. A boy leads one of the boys over to the girls. Katinorodí refuses to go and Kayolí sends the foreign girl to him again and again. The foreign girl insists that JH fetch Katinorodí, but he refuses to come because he is afraid the missionary would see his scratched face (since a scratched face is a typical sign of intercourse). Waidolkáchigi and Kovyoró now leave their sleeping partners because they are scratched up. The foreign girl says angrily: "They wanted to mount us!" Now there is a general fight in which the girls' sleeping skins and blankets are taken by the boys. Yatákana is hit, weeps, and goes to her grandmother. The boys complain of the scratching, and the girls admit that they scratched them.

When the boys have formed a group by themselves, Kuwasiñítn mounts and masturbates on the supine Darotoyí. When Darotoyí goes home Kuwasiñítn masturbates on Nakínak, who is on top of Wetél. Wetél is found weeping near the girls during the night. Darotoyí hovers on the edge of the boys. He does not want to go home. Now he lies down and Kuwasiñítn masturbates on him. Then Maralú comes along, and in falling on Suvyaraikítn he pushes Kuwasiñítn, who pushes Darotoyí so that he rolls off the sleeping skins to the ground. . . . Boys and girls quiet down and the boys join the girls. Katinorodí says to JH that he will not take a sleeping partner among the girls. Kayolí and the foreign girl come and pull him down to the ground by the hair. He stays under the covers

[29] Visitor from another village. He is about 14 years old.
[30] A visitor, age 9 years.
[31] About 7 years old.

with his partner for a while, but later in the night he is back with Suvyaraikítn.[32]

Thus in everyday life *there is a constant veering between sexuality and violence, and often the two are inextricably blended.* An examination of the experimental material from this point of view seems pertinent. Before going ahead, however, we should like to point out that it has always seemed to us that for the children sexual intercourse itself has a certain hostile component. This may readily be inferred from the foregoing data. There are, however, many other indications of the way in which the sexual act and hostility are blended in the minds of the children. A common threat is: "I'll have intercourse with you" and it passes from girl to girl as well as from boy to boy and boy to girl. The boys speak of successful entry as: "I hit it" (as with a projectile), and failure to enter as "I missed it." The little girls (and, indeed, the adults too) believe that menstruation is caused by violent entrance of the vagina; and it can be seen that they scratch the little boys when they attempt intercourse. The great extent to which violence is associated with the sexual act leads to such angry remarks as that of the little foreign girl: "They wanted to mount us!"

In view of this situation we have often been tempted to list every act representative of intercourse in the experiments as hostile. We have refrained, however, because we preferred to limit ourselves to acts obviously hostile in intent. Intercourse has been listed as a hostile act only where it is obviously so from the context, i.e., where it is accompanied by a derogatory remark or where the dolls are made to copulate very violently.

In our experiments there is a great deal of sexual as well as hostile activity. This is due to the fact that the experiment was set up not only in response to the needs of a specific problem, but also in response to the children's spontaneous demands on the material. In so far as experiments permitting spontaneous expression of drives are faithful mirrors of reality, we have much to gain by this procedure. Child life does not usually express itself in terms of one component only; besides, life is full of distractions and alternatives. One of these among the Pilagá is sexual activity. An analysis of a few experiments will illustrate the blending of sexuality and hostility.

Mátakana Trial III puts the baby doll on top of the mother doll and says, "You have intercourse in the anus." By having the baby doll copulate in the anus with the mother doll Mátakana gets the baby away from the breast; expresses contempt for her mother by referring to her vagina as an anus, and insults her baby brother by accusing him of anal intercourse. These are common forms of insult among young and old. A similar purpose is accomplished by placing the baby doll in a sexual position on the father doll, for it gets the baby away from the mother and scornfully implies homosexual activity.

The blending of hostility and sexuality is transparent in Yorodaikolík Trial IV. When Darotoyí puts the Tapáñi doll on the Yorodaikolík doll, Yorodaikolík promptly says: "She's deflowered," i.e., her vagina has been attacked and injured. Later in the same trial after hostile activity with the turtle he puts the sister doll next to his own real penis and then puts the self and sister dolls in copulating position.

Yorodaikolík provides us with many interesting examples of the way in which overt hostility passes easily into overt sexuality and vice versa. Thus, in Trial III he is shaking his fist at the mother doll, but as soon as Simíti puts the Yorodaikolík doll between the legs of the mother doll he says: "Intercourse" and repeats the activity after her. In Trial VI he makes mother and baby dolls copulate; then he switches to murderous activity with a knife, but as soon as it is taken away he changes immediately back to sexual activity. In Trial XI the falling of the sister doll on the self doll at once suggests her death *and* intercourse, and starts a sequence of frantic piling of the dolls one on top of the other. The inner significance of this piling is intercourse, and the piling terminates with the crowning of the heap with a scissors and the announcement that "It has teeth." In Trial XII a long series of hostile acts, some of which have clearcut sexual components, is followed by frank sexual activity and then a sudden switch to hostility again.

Maralú shows an almost constant alternation between transparently hostile acts and sexual ones. Thus, after putting the mother and father dolls in position of intercourse he runs the toy tank[33] over them. Then he amputates the father doll, and after replacing the parts swings the doll in the way that is typical of the child custom of torturing the young of some animal—usually a bird—to death. Then, after improving the shape of the father doll's penis, Maralú again puts the mother and father dolls in position of intercourse.

Another interesting blending of hostility and sexuality is provided by Yatákana, Trial IV, where she pushes the father doll violently on the mother doll in the position of intercourse.

The experiment in which Nakínak, Kuwasiñítn, Wetél, and Yorodaikolík take part is striking in its tremendous release of sexuality. The

---

[33] We had explained to the children the function of a tank.

activity is about equally divided between hetero- and homosexual. Much of it is hostile in intent, that is, most of it consists of insulting references to sexual relations in Nakínak's family. This activity is interpreted as hostile also by Nakínak. Thus, when Wetél puts the brother doll on the mother doll Nakínak takes it off scowling. Later, when Wetél puts the penis of the Nakínak doll into the anus of the brother doll, Nakínak pinches Yorodaikolík for saying "They are having intercourse in the anus." Toward the end of the experiment, when Kuwasiñítn places the brother doll on top of the copulating mother and father dolls Nakínak shakes the box. Previously he had done the same thing himself.

These examples will suffice to indicate the general character of some of the psychic forces at work in the children's play. Hostile and sexual activity alternate with each other, and are sometimes blended in the same act. In discussing inhibition of hostility in the Pilagá experiments, therefore, we must take into account not only the deference of Pilagá children to the dolls as our property, the sanctions against attacking relatives, and the absence of attempts to activate and encourage their attacks on the dolls; but also the fact that the children were free to divert their activity into other channels.

REGRESSION, EXULTATION, SELF-REGARD

REGRESSION

Putting the self doll to nurse is the commonest form of regressive behavior. It occurs in seven cases and is not limited only to children who have younger siblings. We have included in regressive acts not only putting the self doll to nurse, but also placing the self doll next to the mother doll. Regressive behavior occurs in the experiments in the following children: Tapáñi (Trials I, II, III (3 times), IX); Yorodaikolík (Trials I, II, III, XII); Dañakána (Trials III, V); Wetél (Trial I); Naichó (Trials I, II, III); Tanorowí (Trial I); Koitaháa (Trial II). It will be observed that there are no age limits in the group of regressive children. Tapáñi is 8, Yorodaikolík is 4, Dañakána, Wetél, and Naichó are 6, Tanorowí is 10, and Koitaháa is 3. Order of birth has no effect on the appearance of regressive traits. Thus the Pilagá children who manifest symptoms of regression show the following birth sequences: second of three, 2 cases; oldest of three, 1 case; youngest of two, 3 cases; youngset of three, 1 case; oldest of two, 1 case; third of four, 1 case. The number of children in each category has no statistical significance because of the generally small number of cases. In the experiments girls show about the same tendency to regress as boys.

Children with regressive tendencies do not always manifest them in the experiments. Thus, for example, Yatákana, who was continually trying to uncover ZH's breasts, shows no regressive acts in her experiments. Kayolí, another child with strong regressive tendencies in real life, shows no regressive behavior in her experiments. On the other hand there are two children, Wetél, and Tanorowí, who show regressive behavior in the experiments but for whom we have no parallel data from everyday life. In the cases of Wetél and Tanorowí this may be due in part to lack of opportunity to observe these children, who lived at the other end of the village. Four children showed symptoms of regression both in everyday life and in the experiments. Thus, there is evidence of regressive tendencies in nine children.

In the experiments the three children showing the strongest symptoms of regression are Tapáñi, Yorodaikolík, and Naichó, approximately in the order named.

Yorodaikolík's most typical form of regressive behavior in everyday life is climbing into his baby brother's cradle. The following two examples of regressive behavior are, however, of a different character.

1) Diwá'i is standing near our tent with Yorodaikolík on her hip. He is holding one of her breasts and sucks her shoulder.

2) Yorodaikolík tries to put his mother's nipple into an empty cartridge, until his mother gently, and with a smile, pushes him away. Then he tries to roll the cartridge up in her skirt. She does not interfere.

The first example seems almost provocative on Diwá'i's part, for the position on the hip with legs straddled is the position for carrying infants. In Trials I and III Yorodaikolík makes bodily movements frankly expressive of the desire to nurse. In Trial II he limits himself to putting the self doll to nurse. In Trial XII he puts an extra nipple on the mother doll's breast.

Naichó, the deaf and dumb girl, is a last child, and her mother has been dead about four years. In everyday life her overt symptoms of regression were limited to attempts to uncover ZH's breasts; and in her experiments to putting the self doll to nurse.

In the following extract from our field notes Dañakána, Kayolí, and Yatákana can be seen attempting to recapture the position of nurslings.

Dañakána, Kayolí, Yatákana, and a number of little girls from other villages are sitting around ZH, some of them on her lap. Dañakána asks to be taken in ZH's arms. She tries to push the other little girls away. Then she says she is going to nurse, and puts her mouth against ZH's breast. She clasps ZH tightly and calls her *chidéna*, my own mother. After a long while she says, "Well, I'm going home, worse luck." Just then Kayolí comes along and wants to take Dañakána's place on ZH's lap. Dañakána does not go away. She says she will remain where she is. At last she gets up and calls Kayolí *paráchigi laité*, dirty eyes. Kayolí now embraces ZH, says she is going to nurse, and puts her mouth against ZH's breast. Meanwhile Yatákana holds on to ZH tightly. She takes one of ZH's arms and hauls it around her own waist, clutching ZH all the time. Dañakána is boxing, but stops every once in awhile to run over to ZH and Kayolí and call Kayolí "dirty eyes." Yatákana gets up for a moment to box but quickly returns to ZH. But then Dañakána comes over and pushes her away. Kayolí says: "She's chasing you away." Yatákana moves off, but ZH takes her hand and sets her down beside her. Yatákana clutches ZH's hand and does not relinquish it until ZH later goes into the house. Kayolí also holds on to ZH and asks her to keep her arm around her. She calls ZH "my own mother" and asks if she can sleep with her at night. The other little girls want to do the same thing. ZH says that her bed is too narrow. Kayolí turns to the others, and says in a tone of impatience: "That's right, her bed *is* too narrow."

Tapáñi, who shows such obvious symptoms of regression in her doll play (see Trials I, II, III, and IX) shows striking symptoms of regression in everyday life. Among these are her exaggerated baby talk and her tendency to tantrums (Henry (6) and (7)).

EXULTATION

In some of Levy's cases, "after demolition of the baby, the child ran around the room shouting in an exultant manner." Levy made the suggestion that this "activity apparently represented satisfaction of victory—successful completion of an impulse. At the same time, it appeared like a defiant gesture, a defensive form of reaction, a point that needs elaboration through further study."[34] In none of the Pilagá cases did exultation reach such a pitch as to cause the child to run around the room. Nevertheless there were four cases in which attacks on the dolls were accompanied by exultant feelings. Thus, in Darotoyí Trial I, the biting of the turtle is accompanied by exultant verbalization: he has the turtle bite the father doll and says: "Look, it bit his eyes. It's already swallowed them." He next has the turtle bite the brother doll's penis, and says: "Look, it swallowed Kanaidí's penis." In Trial IV, when the turtle bites, Darotoyí cries: "It bit Kanaidí, it bit Kanaidí, it bit Kanaidí, it bit Kanaidí. My father is bitten." Then, when the turtle bites the sister doll he cries: "*Kum!* Her vagina!" All of his subsequent activity in this trial is accompanied by similar verbalization.

It seems unlikely that in this case the exultation is defiant or defensive. It seems rather to represent purely a pleasurable reaction to a vengeful attack that has been successful. It will be observed that there are no evidences of guilt feelings or of fear of retaliation in these trials.

The same seems to be true of Yorodaikolík's exultation in Trial XII where, after blinding the sister doll, he cries: "Oh *way!* Blind!" A similar attitude appears in Denikí Trial VI where he exults as he attempts to amputate the arm of the sister doll.

Dañakána, our quietest child, exults, however, as the turtle bites the sister doll. She cries: "Look, it bit Simíti"; and again, "Ha! Simíti."

Thus, in the Pilagá cases, the exultation seems to represent pleasure in a rather thoroughgoing way, and does not appear to contain fear elements. This does not mean, of course, that attacks are always accompanied by pleasurable feelings unmixed with fear of retaliation.[35]

[34] Levy (10), p. 64.
[35] See, for example, *ibid.*

We have classified under this heading all activity that shows *preoccupation* with the self doll. The cases range from extreme preoccupation with the self doll and open admiration of the self doll, to a mere preoccupation with play between self doll and turtle.

It is striking that the child whose trials show the greatest amount of self-regarding behavior is Tapáñi, one of the *most* disturbed and unhappy children in the group. In Trial I when the examiner asks Tapáñi whether the turtle has bitten her she says: "No. It likes me." In Trial III she puts the self doll on her lap and covers it with her dress. In Trial VI she picks up the self doll and says: "*hayîm onaraili*, I'm a cute and beautiful little thing."[36] In Trial VII the number of times the turtle moves against the self doll is greater than the moves against all of the other dolls put together. If we include the amount of tender care bestowed on the self doll in putting it to nurse in Trials II and III, the number of this type of act is seen to mount even higher.

The child showing the next highest amount of this type of behavior is Dañakána, probably the *least* disturbed child in the village. In Trial III she puts all the dolls on the ground except the self doll, which she keeps on the play table, and says: "Only I remain here." Then, after setting the other dolls up in walking position, she encircles the self doll on the box with her arms. This is followed by a long series of movements with the self doll. In Trial VI she is about to put breasts on the self doll, but stops and puts the self doll alone in the packing case that is serving as play table. Then she puts the plastiline, which was meant to be breasts but has become transformed into a "belt," around the waist of the self doll and keeps it hidden in the box. In Trial VII she asks that the self doll be given a shirt; a little later picks up the self doll and fingers the place where the breasts should be. Then she asks the examiner to draw a picture of her. Finally she turns her back on the sister doll and takes up the self doll, but when JH comes into the house she swiftly seizes the sister doll and puts it back in her hand with the self doll. When JH goes out Dañakána puts the sister doll back. Then she puts the self doll near the sister doll and says: "I know how to dive."

Instances of self-regarding behavior occur in the play of other children also. In Trial IV Yatákana says: "I'm a beautiful little thing." In Trial III Sorói says of the smallest doll: "The cute little thing." This may not have reference to herself, for in this trial the dolls are not named. In the

---

[36] This is said of babies and of individuals whose behavior is approved.

preceding trials, however, the smallest doll has been the self doll. In Trial I Lawésakachiyi puts the largest penis on the self doll. Tanorowí in Trial I permits another girl to take all the dolls but insists on retaining the self doll, saying: "It stays with me." Similar behavior is shown by Koitaháa in Trial II, where he refuses to relinquish the self doll, insisting all the time that "It is not here." In Trial VI Kayolí makes plastiline breasts for *herself* and says: "The same as Simíti's cute little breasts." In Trial IV Yorodaikolík puts aside all the dolls but the self doll, saying: "They are far away." Then the turtle bites the self doll over and over again. This type of behavior with the turtle occurs earlier in the same trial and also in Trial VIII. Darotoyí shows a certain amount of preoccupation with the self in Trial V where he has the turtle bite the self repeatedly and laughs. The first thing that Anetolí does in Trial II is put huge, well-shaped breasts on the self doll. She then says: "Its breasts are huge." Mátakana at one point in Trial II holds the self doll and ignores the sister doll. A striking example of interest in the self doll is provided by Denikí in Trial IV, where he picks up the self doll, holds it to his face, and crows delightedly.

This behavior can be interpreted as serving various functions in the psychic life of the child, and as expressing quite a number of preoccupations. The feeling of not being wanted and of being of little account is compensated for in such expressions as "I'm a cute and beautiful little thing," and in the great amount of tender care bestowed on the self doll. The desire to exclude the deprecating and persecuting environment and be absolutely alone is expressed transparently in such maneuvers as Dañakána's in Trial III and Yorodaikolík's in Trial IV. A similar orientation seems expressed in the self turtle moves—the self doll and turtle form a self-contained little cell from which the turtle emerges to attack the unfriendly environment. Sometimes the preoccupation with the self appears in the manifestation of one of the strong and contradictory wishes of the children—the desire to be an infant, as in Tapáñi II and III, and the desire to be an adult, as in Lawésakachiyi I, or as in Dañakána VI and Anetolí II. Thus these acts would seem to express reaction against rejection, and the contradictory desires to be an infant and to be an adult: they would thus represent the child's struggle to attain some kind of psychic stability.

In the group of children showing this play behavior there are eight girls but only four boys.

IV. BEHAVIOR PROBLEMS[1]

SOME obvious differences between Pilagá culture and our own make clear why we have not discussed certain of Levy's results. There are many child problems in our culture which simply are not problems at all to the Pilagá. Sibling rivalry itself is not considered a problem by the Pilagá in the sense that they believe a child ill if he suffers from it. They are aware that sibling rivalry exists and are careful to keep the sibling away from the newborn infant. They also tell him that if he insists on nursing, the baby will die. But no palliative measures are taken, and sibling rivalry grows to full bloom.

In Pilagá culture "teasing behavior"[2] is rare, and is certainly nothing the parents ever take cognizance of.

"Dreamy and inattentive"[3] behavior never could concern the Pilagá even if it occurred. Attentiveness is not a thing they value, for there is little for adults to concentrate on, and less for children.

No boys have "feminine mannerisms and interests."[4] Although there are certain differences between the behavior of boys and girls, the differences are not sharp before the age of 9 or 10. Boys of less than 10 years are too young to fish, and may go for wild fruit just as girls do. Fetching water is women's (and little girls') work, and we have seen little boys do it only when they are ordered to do so by some young man to whom they are temporarily acting as servants in exchange for *yerba mate*. Although boys are on the whole more aggressive in sex than girls, there is considerable variation. Neither sex, however, could be termed "passive." The sharpest difference between the behavior of little boys and little girls is in the use of dolls. Among the Pilagá, dolls are girls' play, and we have never seen boys even touch them, although the four-year-olds will sometimes watch the girls. A 13 year old boy was referred to Levy for feminine mannerisms and interests. Pilagá boys of that age, however, are well on toward adult participation in the culture. We have never seen any Pilagá adult male display feminine interests. Feminine mannerisms would be most obvious in the use of female speech forms and laughter, but we never saw, nor, indeed, ever heard of a male indulging in these things. Females drop intervocalic *r*, and frequently substitute a glottal stop[5] for a *k* when

---

[1] Detailed discussion of why Pilagá children do not have certain problems which our children have will be reserved for a later publication.

[2] Levy, op. cit., p. 13.

[3] Ibid., p. 14.

[4] Ibid., p. 15.

[5] A slight audible catch in the throat.

they talk, but we have heard this only once in male speech—in a child of three and a half years.[6] The feminine laugh is definitely formalized: it begins with *haj haï haï haï* uttered in rapid succession, mounting toward a loud, musical, and gay cry on the last syllable. None of these things are ever adopted by males.

On the whole, girls have more to gain by being boys than vice versa. If a girl were a boy she would grow into all the prestige patterns of the society, whereas all a boy could have by being a girl would be breasts. Male war and prestige patterns are not so exacting that withdrawal from male activities through becoming a woman would have any advantages. Occasionally there are forthright expressions of penis and breast envy on the part of children (discussed in the section on sexuality), but these do not interfere with adjustment.

We may now consider the behavior problems in Levy's Table VII.[7] One of Levy's cases was referred to him for 'thumbsucking.' Pilagá children, however, do not suck their thumbs. As a matter of fact, the kind of finger-sucking that worries parents and physicians in our culture does not occur among the Pilagá at all. Pilagá children suck and mouth almost anything at all, from their fingers to empty cartridges or razor blades discarded by the ethnologist, but the rhythmic, narcotic-like sucking of the thumb that occurs among children in our culture is not seen among Pilagá children. What sucking of the fingers and mouthing of objects does occur among them is not considered improper by the adults; nor do they recognize it as a dangerous habit that may interfere with proper social adjustment.

Pilagá children do not imitate their older siblings. In our culture such imitation is often based on some consistent favoritism shown the older sibling, but it is always the younger sibling who is favored among the Pilagá.

Although Pilagá children have temper tantrums they could not be classified as "temper-tantrum children." Of the ordinary "run of the mill" tantrum, arising from a momentary frustration or upset, we have a few examples. These ordinary tantrums must be distinguished from the *séwat*, the "left behind" tantrum that occurs when a child's mother leaves the village to go for wood, water, or forest fruits. This latter type of tantrum is hysterical. The following are a few examples of ordinary tantrums.

---

[6] He would quite naturally tend to imitate his mother.

[7] This table lists the 12 cases discussed by Levy in his monograph together with the particular problems for which they were referred to him. See op. cit., p. 35.

1) Yorodaikolík is weeping because, say the children, Denikí has hit him. Denikí, they say, is *kalawaráik*, violent. When Yorodaikolík goes home his mother stretches out her hand to him. When he goes to her she wipes his face. Denikí strikes her, and throws himself back in a trantrum. When the mother finishes washing Yorodaikolík's face he quiets down. Then she picks up Denikí, who is still lying on the ground weeping, and she starts to wash his face. He screeches. When she has finished she nurses him and he becomes quiet.

This is a symmetrical reaction to the rivalry situation. The tantrum is easily quieted, and no punishment is administered.

2) ZH gives a picture book to Yorodaikolík. When Naichó takes it away from him he falls down weeping. His mother and Araná tell him to be quiet. When his mother picks him up, places him on her lap, and wipes his eyes with the heel of her hand he stops crying. He remains on her lap.

Yorodaikolík's tantrum is immediately quieted through the highly standardized technique of wiping the eyes with the heel of the hand. Much of what would be more elaborate solicitude in our own culture is standardized among the Pilagá into such impersonal, perfunctory movements as wiping a child's eyes with the heel of the hand or delousing him. Note that after gaining the coveted position on his mother's lap Yorodaikolík remained there.

3) Naichó screamed in temper when she did not get her shell filled with cooked flour. Immediately her grandmother and then Nenarachí offered theirs to her. She refused. Then they sent her to another member of the household and she was fed.

4) Naichó screaming for food. Her grandmother puts her arms around the child, saying: "Look, your older sister," and gives her a dish of flour cooked in water. Naichó stops weeping.

In these four examples it is clear that the tantrum is used to get something out of the environment. Sometimes, however, the child miscalculates.

5) Yorodaikolík is weeping because, they say, his mother wants to bathe him. He comes out of the house and deliberately stirs up and steps on the household store of wild fruit that is drying on the ground in the sun. His mother comes out and tries to drag him away. He falls down in a tantrum. Tapáñi comes out of the house and strikes him on the back. He weeps more loudly. His mother drags him off to one side and bathes him from a small pot of water.

6) Diwá'i and Araná start out to sell their grass. Tapáñi follows them screaming at the top of her voice. Diwá'i has struck Tapáñi. When Tapáñi continues to follow, Araná turns round and scolds her, telling her

to go home. When Tapáñi keeps on coming Diwá'i picks up a stick and throws it at Tapáñi, who dodges. She stops for a moment, but then continues to follow, screaming all the while.

It is somewhat doubtful whether the *séwat* really belongs in the tantrum category. Whereas tantrums are used to oblige the environment to yield, the *séwat* seems to stem from strong disruptive forces in the child's personality. When the child sees its mother leave the village it must mean to him: (1) The desertion he constantly expects because in general his mother is not warm and loving and (2) the desertion he fears because of his hostile impulses toward her; (3) rejection with which she constantly threatens him if he makes too much of a nuisance of himself. The adult Pilagá reaction to the *séwat* outburst is frequently violent: the adults become irritated and treat the child harshly.

7) Diwá'i (their mother) gets up to go out of the house. Denikí and Yorodaikolík weep frantically. Yorodaikolík starts to follow his mother and the people in the house say: "You're lost." He continues to follow and runs in front of her. JH cannot see what is happening because they are far away and Diwá'i is carrying a big load of grass. JH at last gets close enough to see him catch hold of Diwá'i but she pushes him off and he falls to the ground. Yalákachitn picks him up screaming and kicking and carries him home like a sack. She lays him on the ground where he lies screaming, so she deprives him of his little woven bag, taking it from around his neck. Denikí toddles over from Sutaráina, and Yalákachitn picks him up. Later JH sees Denikí with the bag. Sutaráina picks up Yorodaikolík by the hand and says to him: "She'll be back later." Ten minutes later he is still weeping.

8) Kapíetn is screaming. They say it is because he wants his mother. JH takes his hand and leads him, without any trouble, to his sister, Lorosétina. She tells him to be quiet. He screams and screams, and she hits him several times on the mouth. He continues to scream. She tries to distract his attention by pointing out JH, but he continues to scream. At last his mother returns and picks him up. He quiets instantly. She nurses him.

9) Diwá'i leaves the fish trap to take fish home. Yorodaikolík clings to her. She drags him over to Waik who holds him while he screams and throws himself back in his efforts to get away. Waik keeps repeating: "She'll be back later," but Yorodaikolík continues. At last Waik lets him loose. Sidingkí sets him on his lap and comforts him.

10) Yorodaikolík is frantic and clings to his mother when she wants to go for palm shoots. Sutaráina drags him off and beats him. Diwá'i says, angrily: "The deuce take him. Stay here!"

11) Kapíetn's mother and Kayolí go for water. Kapíetn screeches as if his lungs would burst. At last Kaláchiyolí drags him over to the shade house. Now Ñorol'í holds him in her arms, but he keeps right on screaming. Kaláchiyolí says to ZH, within earshot of Kapíetn, that Kapíetn's mother has "thrown him away because she is fed-up with him." When Kapíetn continues to weep Kaláchiyolí takes him away from Ñorol'í and ties his hands together with a belt. She ties them over and over. Kapíetn lies on the ground, and Ñorol'í walks over to him in a leisurely manner, unties his hands, and puts him on her lap again. He continues shrieking: "Mother! Mother!"

These examples will suffice to illustrate the character of the *séwat*. It seems that although the children have the constant experience of temporary disappearance and later return of the mother, each time the mother goes it represents a threat of utter deprivation, with consequent emotional collapse. The mothers are irritated by the hysterical clinging of the children; and the other members of the household range in reaction from annoyance to perfunctory care. Schematically the picture is: the departing and irritated mother, the frantic child, and the violent or perfunctorily comforting housemate. Thus, extreme distress in a child frequently drives adults to acts of violence. To the Pilagá these instances of breakdown are merely temporary and well-recognized phases of child behavior, irritating it is true, but not serious.

A Pilagá child never refuses food except in a temporary pet. These are rare. When he refuses no one coaxes him, and he comes and eats after awhile.

Baby-talk is recognized as a way young children talk. It is not a sign of mental illness to the Pilagá. Occasionally one finds a woman who still makes the substitution of *w* for *l* that is characteristic of child speech, but all males and almost all females outgrow their baby-talk. No Pilagá children stammer—their speech disturbances take a different form.[8]

Pilagá children do not vomit unless they are seriously ill.

The quarreling of their children constitutes no problem to the Pilagá. Sometimes the adults take sides in the quarrels, sometimes they stimulate them, at times they counsel the children to be quiet, more often they ignore them.

Pilagá children do not have night terrors. This is very striking. Although we lived in great intimacy with the Pilagá, and had for neighbors some of the most disturbed children, there was no evidence of night terrors.

[8] See Henry (6). In that publication we pointed out that speech disturbances in Pilagá children range from exaggeration and prolongation of baby-talk to neurotic deafness and dumbness.

The children constantly strive for attention, but they do not make a special point of doing it when the baby is being nursed.

Pilagá children are never negativistic or destructive. Regressive behavior is a common trait of Pilagá childhood but it passes almost unnoticed by the adults.

Thus, most of the behavior traits which, in our society, lead a thoughtful parent to consider a child in need of psychiatric care, either do not occur or are ignored among the Pilagá. The question naturally arises whether the Pilagá recognize mental illness in children at all. The answer is that they do—in their way. Like so many parents in our culture, they consider that children who show *extreme* or *unusual* behavior are bad children, not sick ones. A Pilagá child who is more violent than the others, or greedier than the others, is a bad child. One who is competitive in a noncompetitive game is a bad child; and a child who has serious speech disturbances is ridiculous and contemptible.

We have one case of a child who was considered "sick" because of extreme behavior, but it was during only a moment of the child's life, and it was an extreme case. We give the data below.

Denikí is weeping outside the house. The people inside call out: "Go away from him." This is in order to frighten him with the threat of desertion by his mother, in the fantastic hope that the fear will make him stop crying. Someone else calls out: "A cannibal is coming." This again is to frighten him into stopping his crying, or into going inside the house to his mother. Meanwhile no one comes out to him. He stands outside weeping for perhaps another five minutes. Then he goes inside and approaches his mother, who sits with her hand outstretched to him. He backs away from her, pushing himself on his buttocks, until he stops behind a post. Tapáñi is about to go and get him, when Nenarachí says: "Scare him." So Tapáñi goes outside the house, comes up behind Denikí, and makes a noise by rustling the leaves in the house wall. Meanwhile someone says: "It's an old hag." (Old hags are supposed to want to bite children.) The baby flees weeping to its mother. He nurses for about twenty seconds, leaps up, and returns to the place behind the post. Then he goes outside. No one moves. He comes back, goes to his mother, who sits smiling with outstretched hand, nurses for twenty seconds, and again leaps up and goes outside. He runs away a little, but again returns to his mother and nurses. Again he leaps up and flees outside. His mother follows him outside and stretches out her hand. The baby is sitting on the ground screaming. His mother returns to the house, and the baby flees toward the path leading out of the village. Nagête goes toward him, but Naichó picks him up and puts him on her hip. Nagête tries to take the baby from Naichó, and when Naichó resists Nagête tears the baby out of her arms. The baby's screaming intensifies and then quiets. He straightens his legs and stretches his arms, showing his desire to descend. Nagête takes him into the house to his mother, who puts him in her carrying band, and then to her breast. Piyarasáina says: "He's sick." Someone else says: "He's angry." Baby nurses quietly.

Here the outraged and desperate infant has finally forced the callous adults into activity, and even into worry. His behavior was extreme, and not duplicated by himself or by any other child while we were among the Pilagá. It is clear that where only extreme suffering is taken as the criterion of illness, whole areas of maladjustment must be ignored.

In considering Pilagá indifference to maladjustment in children it must also be borne in mind that although they ignore symptoms, this is not an unmitigated evil, for, if they do not try to heal, *neither do they attempt to punish.* Sucking the finger and all kinds of other objects, quarreling, baby-talk, and regression, the commonest symptoms of maladjustment in Pilagá children, go unpunished. Hence the problems do not become intensified. Punishment is likely to come only in the *séwat* situation.

V. SEXUALITY

WHERE children can see the adult sexual act, where sexual conversation and gestures are perfectly open, and child life is untrammeled by sexual taboos, it is reasonable to expect that the children should experiment with their sexual apparatus and attempt to imitate adult sexual behavior. This is the case among the Pilagá. Considering the extent of child knowledge about sex and the age at which this knowledge becomes articulate—3 years—intercourse in a Pilagá household must not only be visible to the children, but carried on with little if any attempt to conceal the act from them. Absolutely no prohibition is placed on child sexual activity by the adults, so that the children are at liberty to do what they please. Under such circumstances the only limits to the child's sexual activity are his physiological capacities and the tolerance of his companions.

It must be clear from the previous sections that sex is a strong and constant interest of Pilagá children. It is the purpose of this section to consider those aspects of sexual behavior which appear in the experiments and to relate them to day-by-day observation.

The commonest forms of sexual activity with the dolls—activity not directly related, however, to the standard play procedure of placing proper genitals on the dolls, in order of frequency, are: 1) placing the dolls in position of intercourse; 2) castration; 3) change of sex. Other forms of activity are: 4) piling; 5) the making of penises that look like breasts. In one trial Sorói repeatedly changed the form of the plastiline from penis to breast and back again. Throughout the play verbalization often makes clear the intent of the activity listed as sexual.

The psychoanalyst would no doubt go much further than we have in analysis of this activity. Considering the newness of the material and our own lack of psychoanalytic preparation, we have thought it best to limit our discussion to the most obvious aspects of the material.

Intercourse position. The commonest form of sexual activity is placing the mother and father dolls in intercourse position. This was done by ten children. As being the most impressive act on the child's sexual horizon and the one most fraught with consequences and meaning for himself, it is to be expected that most of the children would perform at least this act even if they performed no other.

That the parents' sexual activity is disturbing to the child can be inferred from the following. In Darotoyí Trial I, Yorodaikolík says: "Simkoolí (Darotoyí's baby sister) is crying because her mother is having intercourse." Tanorow'í Trial I points to the self doll and says: "It's crying"; and in answer to the examiner's question, why, she says: "Because they (the parent dolls) are having intercourse." It will be observed that in this trial she stretches the arm of the father doll over the self while the father doll is lying in copulating position on the mother doll. Thus she signifies her desire not to be excluded during the sexual act. A similar and more intense expression of this attitude occurs in her second trial where, after maneuvering the mother and father dolls into a position which to her signifies intercourse, she puts the self doll in the arms of the father doll, the face of the self doll very close to the penis of the father doll.[1] Thus, twice she placed the self doll in position of great intimacy with the father doll while she dramatized the sexual activity of her parents. The subsequent act, in which she places the self doll near the mother doll, with the face of the self doll next to the anal region seems to have been a move preparatory to further movements with the parent dolls.

Tanorowí's activity in these two instances demonstrates the desire to be included within the parents' sphere of interest at all times; and the desire for sexual intimacy with the father. It is interesting that she does not put the self doll directly in position of intercourse with the father doll. The fact that the face of the self doll was placed close to the penis of the father doll may have been due to carelessness in arranging the dolls. Since we do not have in our notes that the move was deliberate, and since, being so rigid, the dolls are not always easy to manage, we cannot be sure that the position of the self doll in this instance really represents oral strivings.

Two other girls gave experimental evidence of desire for sexual relations with the father. In Trial II Dañakána puts the baby doll on the father doll, close to the penis and says: "They're copulating." The examiner asks "Is that it's father?" and Dañakána answers "Yes." The baby doll would, in this case, be Dañakána, because she is the youngest in her family. Besides, she occupies exactly the same position as Sorói who had just been using the dolls, and who had been represented by the same doll. The case of her sister, Simíti is clearer. Even though Simíti does not place the self doll in copulating position with the father doll, she spends practically the whole of her eighth trial manipulating and stroking the penis of the father doll, finally placing the father doll on the mother doll.

Considering the general sexual background, and the way in which Pilagá men hold their children, it would be strange indeed if little girls did not view their fathers as sexual objects. The characteristic way in

---

[1] At this point the reader will naturally be reminded of Melanie Klein's observation that "As a result of the oral frustration the child undergoes it seeks new sources of gratification. The little girl turns away from her mother and takes her father's penis as an object of gratification. At first this gratification is of an oral nature, but there are genital tendencies at work already" (op. cit., p. 210).

which a man holds his child is between his legs. Since often he wears only a breech clout, or sits with his skirt thrown back over his legs, exposing the breech-clout covered penis, it is natural that a little girl should develop an interest in her father's genital.

The desire of a little boy to have intercourse with his mother appears in Darotoyí II, and in Yorodaikolík V, VIII, and IX. Yorodaikolík was once observed to masturbate on the buttocks of his mother who was lying down. She did nothing to stop him. Darotoyí was never observed to do this. In the development of this kind of behavior in little boys a number of factors must be taken into consideration. First is the pregnancy and lactation taboo on intercourse, and the long period of abstinence it imposes on the woman as well as on the man. During this period two women were observed to use the feet of their infant sons to masturbate, i.e., they held the feet of the babies, 8 and 15 months respectively at the time of the observation, pressed against their genitals. Another important factor is that mothers manipulate the genitals of their infant sons. It is likely also that the straddled position of the child on its mother's hip in carrying would have some effect in focusing the child's sexual interests.

In the play of Yorodaikolík one sometimes gets the impression that putting the self doll in copulating position with the mother doll really takes the place of putting the self doll to nurse.[2] It is significant in this connection that Yorodaikolík never puts the self doll to nurse, although in other respects, as we have seen, he has given convincing evidence of his regression wishes. We have no evidence of regression from Darotoyí.

Yorodaikolík's sexual drives, however, are not limited to his mother. He also puts the self doll several times in position of intercourse with the sister doll. In everyday life Yorodaikolík's sexual horizon is far from circumscribed. He utilizes a great deal of his environment for erotic purposes, masturbating not only against his sometimes compliant, sometimes rejecting sister, against Naichó, his housemate, against other little boys and girls in the village, but also against inanimate objects. He manipulates his penis constantly. A generalized erotic attitude toward the environment is also characteristic of the other little boys and girls.[3]

In Trial III Anetolí gives us another interesting insight into the child's attitude toward intercourse of the parents. After putting the mother and father dolls in position of intercourse, the father doll's penis falls off. She remarks: "It's good that way." Castration is a typical form of attack and

---

[2] "A move of this [oral sucking] nature on her [the girl's] part towards the father, and, in the boy, a second orientation towards the mother as a genital love-object, sets up a new aim for the libidinal gratification of the child, in which the genitals begin to make their influence felt." Op. cit., p. 211.

[3] No girl has been observed to use inanimate objects.

may be conceived as serving three functions: the expression of general hostility, the expression of the wish to make sexual relations between the parents impossible, and the expression of penis envy. Sorói in Trial IV squashes the penis of the father doll and leaves it that way. Koitaháa in Trial II asks whether he may remove the penis of the father doll, and when told no, does it anyway. A few moments later in the same trial he says of the father doll: "I burn it." It will be remembered that Koitaháa has a three day old sibling.

Attacks on genitalia. Darotoyí, in a state of high exultation, attacks the genitals of his entire family. In Trial I he attacks the genital of the baby doll, and the penises of the father and brother dolls. He behaves similarly in Trial V, except that he attacks the genital of the older sister and the mother also. Yorodaikolík's remark in Trial IV that the sister doll is deflowered, and his attack on her vagina in Trial VI, are other aspects of the same drive toward attack on the genitals.

Attack on the genitals is the converse of *fear* of attack on the genitals. In everyday life attacks on the genitals—real, feinting, and verbal—are common enough. Below are a few examples.

1) Nagête, playing with Yorodaikolík, pushes him over and handles his penis, saying: "I'll cut it off."

2) Diwá'i screams and screams at Yorodaikolík: "Come here! Come here!" When he does go home his mother, Nenarachí, and Piyärasáina scold him poisonously. Nenarachí says: "You will be killed." Piyärasáina says: "Your penis will be cut off."

3) Araná and Nagête put a dead nestling in Denikí's face. Denikí seems half frightened, half amused. He leans against Nagête's arm. Then she touches his penis and says: "It is bleeding." His penis, however, is not bleeding. Tapáñi says: "It's bleeding." . . . Araná opens the bird's mouth and puts Denikí's penis in it, saying: "It is devoured, it is devoured." Denikí starts to whimper, but does not touch the bird. Either Araná or Nagête at last takes the bird away. Denikí goes out.

4) Yorodaikolík is sitting near the fire. His mother says: "Your testicles." Yorodaikolík moves away. His mother picks up a firebrand and puts it between his legs, moving it toward his genitalia. He immediately bursts into tears and leans on his mother's breast. She strokes his head and he soon stops.

5) Nenarachí says to Simíti: "You'd better guard your vagina, because if you don't a man will come along, take you away and rape you. Then you'll be a poor little thing when your vagina bleeds."

6) Sídingkí makes a jab at Simíti's vulva with a 10 inch hunting knife. She retreats. Sídingkí says to JH: "She's going to show you her genitals."

7) JH offers his watch to Dañakána so that she may listen to the tick. She withholds in embarrassment. JH withdraws the watch. Nagête, Nenarachí, and Piyärasáina insult her in a steady stream until she weeps and goes home. The insult most often repeated is: *nuwáltapïgï sumï lópï mï lat' é segamï kochítl lópï komï kochítl*—she is fed up with her big wormy vagina.

Change of sex. The next problem to consider is the change of sex of the dolls. The sex of the dolls was changed in the following trials: Kayolí V (mother); Dañakána II (father); Anetolí I and III (brothers); Naichó V (father?); Yorodaikolík XII (self and brother). In the cases of Kayolí and Dañakána the activity following the change of genital is too brief to permit an inference as to its possible meaning. In Anetolí's trials the genitals of the dolls are not changed, but breasts are put on male dolls. This activity was carried on in perfect awareness of the sex of the dolls. It will be observed that in the first two trials Anetolí in collaboration with her playmates puts breasts on all the dolls. It is not until well on in the third trial that interest shifts momentarily away from breasts to genitals but ends up with breasts. Although it is true that girls of this age are extremely preoccupied with breasts and the possibility of their having them, it does not seem that this preoccupation is sufficient in itself to explain the persistent drive toward putting breasts on the male dolls. The authors have no specific explanation to offer for which they can produce supporting evidence from everyday life.

Yorodaikolík changes the penises of the self and baby dolls to vulvas in Trial XII. There is some indication that this change of sex is related to his fantasy life, for in another place he gave evidence of breast fantasies. In Tapáñi's Trial VI, when she puts large breasts on the self doll, he points to his own chest and says: "My breasts." Other little Pilagá boys have these fantasies too. Thus, while Darotoyí and Kapíetn were watching the little girls play a sexual game, they repeated over and over again to ZH: *sik'ón yotité*—my breasts hurt.

There is no direct evidence in the experiments that little girls have fantasies regarding their possession of the male organs. No little girl changed the vulva on the self doll to a penis. One child, Kayolí, changed the vulva of the mother doll to a penis. Kayolí is very interesting,[4] not only because she was the only girl to change a female genital to a male

---

[4] For a thorough discussion of the personality of this child see Henry (7).

one, but also because she is the one Pilagá girl we know who gave unmistakable and spontaneous evidence of desire to possess the male organ. Thus, one day, she improvised the following little song:

yóla	*laitá*
my testicles	their odor
ñikowí	*laitá*
my penis	its odor
yópï	*laitá*
my vagina	its odor
ñaté	*laitá*
my buttocks	their odor

Kayolí was also the inventor of the Matagói raping-game. In this game she impersonated Matagói, a maladjusted adolescent boy, who for some weeks was the hero of the children of our village because of his depredations on the mission store. But since he persisted in his robberies, and also quarreled with his family, the older Pilagá were frankly annoyed with him and called him *haláraik*, lunatic. Rape is a trait of *haláraiks*, and hence Kayolí called herself Matagói when she went on a "raping" rampage. Even though Matagói was never accused of rape he was considered capable of it because he was *haláraik*. The following is an example of Kayolí's "raping behavior":

With her skirt parted in front and raised to expose her vulva, Kayolí chases the little girls around the village compound. When she catches one she makes rhythmic movements of intercourse against her, lifting the girl's skirt and exposing her vulva, which the child then covers with her hands. JH goes into the house to write, and Kayolí comes in after him. Tapáñi starts to enter and Kayolí makes a grab for her. Tapáñi first retreats but then comes in. Kayolí raises Tapáñi's skirt to the level of her vulva and makes rhythmic movements against Tapáñi's rump, as Tapáñi covers her vulva with her hands.

The following note is from an early stage in our field work, when the children were as yet unidentified. It is another example of a penis fantasy in a little girl. Unfortunately we do not know who it is.

A girl of 7 is chasing two boys the same age. She is holding a piece of rubber tube which she calls a penis. When the ethnologist asks her whether it is her penis, she answers: "No." The following conversation takes place: Ethnologist: "Would you like to have one?" "No." E.: "Perhaps you have a vagina and a penis." "No."

Breast-like penises were made for male dolls by Wetél II, Sorói V, and Tanorowí II. Since Pilagá children are excellent modelers in clay, the breast-like appearance of the penis cannot be ascribed to lack of control of the material. It should also be noted that although Wetél put a breast-like genital on the father doll he put a well-shaped penis on the self doll; and that after putting a breast-like penis on the brother doll, Sorói put a perfectly definite vulva on the self doll.

It is obvious that we are face to face with a definite problem, but one which, for reasons previously given, cannot be solved here. It is suggested that this behavior is functionally related to: (1) phases of libidinal development described by Melanie Klein in the note already quoted; 2) the desire to exclude the father from the circle of the mother's interest; 3) hostile impulses centering around the removal of the dominating males. Sorói's repeated change of penis to breasts to penis in Trial VI is probably related to the first.

Spread of sexuality. Two children, Yorodaikolík and Mátakana, piled the dolls on top of one another. In this activity we may see the kind of *spread of a drive* which Levy pointed out in another context[5] In Yorodaikolík's trials the activity has a sexual meaning, and may be related to the habit young Pilagá children have of piling one on top of the other in a frenzy of masturbation. In the case of Mátakana it is not clear that the piling activity has a sexual meaning. In this type of behavior with the dolls the child appears carried away by the power of the drive so that he pushes on in the same way with all the objects at his disposal. Yorodaikolík even treats the scissors as something human.

Spread of the sexual drive can be seen not only in the play of Yorodaikolík and Mátakana, but also in that of Darotoyí. The spread, however, does not always consist in piling. It often extends laterally to other objects. Thus, for example, in the play of Yorodaikolík he at times achieves a large number of lateral combinations. In Trial IX the mother is placed face downward on all of the dolls at once and Yorodaikolík says: "Look! Intercourse." Then he puts the self doll on the mother doll; then the baby doll on the sister doll and then on the mother dolls, saying: "Has intercourse." He ends by placing the self doll on the sister doll and says: "Has intercourse." In XII his placing of the sister doll on the mother doll is merely preliminary to a general piling whose significance is intercourse. A similar situation is presented in VI where he places the baby doll under the mother doll, says: "Intercourse," and at once places the self and sister dolls on the mother doll.

Lateral spread can be observed in Darotoyí II, where, after putting the self doll on the mother and then on the sister dolls he puts the father doll on the brother doll and then on the sister doll. In Mátakana II, after

[5] Op. cit., p. 53. For other examples of this phenomenon see Denikí's trials.

putting the baby doll on the mother doll and saying: "The product of her vagina," she immediately begins to pile all the dolls except the father doll on top of the mother doll. The same move is repeated later in the same trial when, after putting the baby doll to nurse, she places the sister doll on the mother doll, and a few moments later she places the father doll on top of all. In Trial III we observe a lateral spread. After putting the mother doll on the father doll with the remark, "Has intercourse," she puts the baby doll on the mother with the derogatory remark, "You have intercourse in the anus," and transfers the doll to the father doll. After putting the mother doll to her mouth she again puts the baby doll on the father doll, penis to penis. Acts that are similar mechanically, however, are not always similar psychically. Thus, although in Trial II the moves with the baby doll have the meaning of getting the baby out of the way— sending it back where it came from—the movements with the other dolls cannot all be interpreted in that way because the self doll is included. On the other hand, in Trial III the intent seems the same in all cases, the contact of the penises of the baby and father dolls being related to the known homosexuality of little boys. In the play of Darotoyí and Yorodaikolík, however, the spreading has uniformly the significance of intercourse.

The phenomenon of spread of sexuality can be observed also in the experiment in which Nakínak, Kuwasiñítn, Wetél, and Yorodaikolík took part. Thus, Nakínak puts the brother doll on top of the copulating mother and father dolls, and Kuwasiñítn does the same thing immediately after him.

In the experiment last mentioned there is so much homosexual activity that it seems worth while to include some more observations from everyday life of little boys.

Kapíetn pulls his penis into erection. Kuwasiñítn has been putting his fingers into Kapíetn's anus. Kuwasiñítn plays with Kapíetn's penis. Kapíetn goes away but keeps coming back to Kuwasiñítn. Kapíetn lies down on Kuwasiñítn's lap, face down, rubbing his penis on Kuwasiñitn's lap. Yorodaikolík runs over to him and, after pulling back his own foreskin, thrusts his penis into Kapíetn's anus. Kapíetn goes off crying. Darotoyí is leaning on JH's lap, face down. Kuwasiñítn puts his finger into Darotoyí's anus and he starts to cry. Kuwasiñítn goes away and Darotoyí stops crying.

Darotoyí and Yorodaikolík are pressing their penises together. They are laughing and saying they are having intercourse. Meanwhile Kapíetn is pressing against Yorodaikolík's back.

Wetél pulls back Yorodaikolík's foreskin. Yorodaikolík appears to enjoy it.

VI. CONCLUSIONS

THE authors undertook their field research with the object of testing two propositions: (1) That, given similar intra-familial relationships in distinct cultures, the effects of these relationships on the children will be similar. (2) That, wherever sibling rivalry exists the general symptom pattern will be approximately the same.

The study of Pilagá intra-familial relationships shows that under similar conditions of familial tension children in distinct cultures will develop the same kind of symptom patterns.

The study of Pilagá children shows also that the patterns of behavior in sibling rivalry among them follow with little difference those found among children in our own society. The most important difference between the sibling rivalry patterns in our own society and those found among the Pilagá is that among the Pilagá remorse and self-punishment do not occur as consequences of hostility. Inasmuch, however, as remorse and self-punishment, while outstanding as general cultural sanctions in our own culture, do not occur as sanctions in Pilagá culture at all, it must be concluded that the difference in the sibling rivalry pattern between the two cultures is culturally determined. Remorse and self-punishment are not, therefore, fundamental to the sibling rivalry syndrome.

The problem naturally arises as to how far sibling rivalry is itself culturally determined. Since the loss or fear of loss of maternal affection is central to the problem, the question may very well be asked: Would sibling rivalry exist at all where not the mother but several aunts are the desirable objects? Or would it exist where the mother showered attentions equally on both children? Would sibling rivalry exist where the culture as a whole generated little anxiety? Finally, would sibling rivalry exist where membership in an important and wonderful secret society was absolutely contingent on the birth of a younger sibling, so that the presence of a new baby opened a new and wonderful life to the older sibling? Some day ethnologists may be able to study these problems in the field.

As in almost any piece of research, other useful data were obtained incidentally to testing the fundamental hypotheses. Outstanding in this connection is the material related to the experimental procedure itself. Differences in techniques naturally produce different results and turn up different problems. The principal differences between our own and Levy's experimental handling of the problem of sibling rivalry were: 1) Our dolls represented the child's entire family, whereas Levy's always represented the same trio—mother, baby, sibling. 2) Our dolls were named for the child's family, while Levy's dolls were simply "mother," "baby," and "brother," or "sister." 3) Whereas Levy presented his children with a dramatic situation and a problem to solve ("What does she (or he) do?"), neither of these things were done in our experiments. 4) Levy's dolls had no genitals—ours did.

In view of these differences in procedure certain results were almost inevitable. 1) Lacking a dramatic plot and a problem to solve, the children, left to their own devices, played as they would and let their hostility follow along lines determined by their inner needs and by the cultural pattern. 2) Since the children had a clear conception of whom each doll represented they "picked their targets" in accordance with their own inner needs and the cultural patterns. 3) Since the dolls had genitalia, and since play was limited neither by plot nor problem, the children were free to express their sexual drives as well as their hostile and other impulses. This permitted a more complete analysis of behavior patterns than might otherwise have been obtained.

A second finding is that knowledge of the language and culture of a tribe is necessary before valid interpretation of the experimental data from a primitive tribe is possible.

In a culture that still retains the larger part of its old folk ways, and exists relatively isolated from strong influences of white culture, the children either speak their own language exclusively or, even where they can speak the white man's language, favor their own overwhelmingly as an everyday means of communication. It is doubtful that anyone, ignorant of the primitive language, would be so foolhardy as to attempt a study of primitive children who speak no language but their own. There are difficulties, however, even where the children speak the white man's language in addition to their own. Where these cultures are not broken down— and often, indeed, where they are—the children still prefer to use their own language with their own people. Hence in their play, an aspect of their lives which gives so much insight into their personalities, and in their day by day dealings with their parents, they use the native tongue. This shuts the "examiner" out; unless he too talks the native language, the wealth of casual and intimate detail which serves as a background for the interpretation of the experimental results will be lost.

Another factor in this situation is the sociological difficulty created by the language barrier. If the child uses one language when talking to his tribemates, but must use another with the "examiner," the experimental situation becomes distinctly a "white man's situation"; a relationship with an outsider, with whom, however benevolent he may be, one cannot even talk one's own language. This makes the whole situation artificial, and good rapport is hard to achieve.

The last twenty years have witnessed rapid growth in the interest of psychologists and psychiatrists in testing their hypotheses in cultures other than our own. This interest will no doubt continue to grow, for the possibilities offered by such testing are very great. For their part, anthropologists have shown an increasing interest in employing in their field work the techniques of psychology and psychiatry. It is likely that the post war period will see anthropology emerge vigorously from the academic cloisters into the field of practical problems—a field in which anthropologists will not only be asked to study primitive cultures, but to help build them up and absorb them into the stream of world culture. For this high purpose they will need more than ever the techniques of their sister sciences—particularly those of psychology and psychiatry. It is hoped that this monograph will indicate a way in which anthropologists may utilize the tools developed by those other disciplines.

VII. PROTOCOLS OF THE EXPERIMENTS

A TOTAL of 89 experiments, called "trials," were conducted with the children discussed in this monograph. The experimental procedure itself has been described in an earlier section. The procedure followed in presenting the protocols of the experiments is as follows.

1. *Order of presentation.* The protocols have been arranged (a) according to the order in which the children appear on the list of Dramatis Personnae; (b) with siblings grouped together; (c) according to the age of the children. Examples: Naichó appears first because she is the first child listed in house number one in the village. She is followed by Tapáñi, Yorodaikolík, and Deniki because these are the next children listed. Tapáñi, Yorodaikolík, and Deniki are siblings. Tapáñi is the oldest of the three siblings.

2. *Dates.* The date on which each trial was performed is retained in order that the reader may get some idea of the lapse of time between each trial.

3. *Description of conditions.* A description of the general conditions under which the play was conducted is given in the section on Procedure. Whenever necessary, additional material pertinent to the particular trial is incorporated in the body of the protocol. In each trial, for example, it is stated which children were present. In this way the reader may form a more precise idea of the character of the influences operating during the course of the play.

4. *Symbols.* Arabic numerals in parentheses are used to indicate hostile acts. The hostile acts are numbered in succession as they occur in the trials. Italic numerals are used to indicate sexual acts.

5. *Summaries.* The complete set of trials for each child is followed by an analytical summary. These summaries are divided into three sections— Pattern of Hostility, Pattern of Sexual Objects, Other Patterns.

Pattern of Hostility contains three sub-sections: I. Direction. This subsection contains a list of all the trials in numerical order. The words (sister, mother, father, etc.) next to each number indicate, in succession, the dolls toward which hostile acts were directed. Where the number of the trial is omitted no hostile activity took place. II. Forms. This subsection enumerates all the hostile moves in the trials, with their descriptions and the dolls toward which the moves were directed. III. Restitution. This sub-section occurs in order that the reader may make comparison between restitutive acts in the Levy experiments and acts that resemble them in our experiments.

Pattern of Sexual Objects contains two sub-sections. I. Direction. The hyphenated pairs indicate the dolls placed in sexual relationship. II. Forms. The hyphenated pairs indicate the dolls placed in sexual relationship.

Other Patterns. When interesting patterns not provided for under the previous headings occur in the protocols they are summarized in this section.

NAICHÓ[1]

Age: 6
Sex: female
Siblings: Yalákachitn, female, age 30
Nenarachí, female, age 25

Note: Although Naichó is deaf and dumb the examiner had succeeded in eliciting some rudimentary responses to speech. Before beginning the play the examiner named the dolls for Naichó. Naichó's defect, however, necessarily made the extent of her comprehension an open question. In the protocols, therefore, the dolls are numbered and not named. The self doll is #1, Nenarachí is #2, and Yalákachitn is #3. The parent dolls are called mother and father.

Trial I. 10–11–37. All but the father doll have female genitals. The mother doll and the #2 doll have breasts but #1 and #3 have not.

Naichó puts #1 in nursing position against #2. She presses #2 next to father doll. Stands up #2 so that it faces father doll. Lays down #2. Lays mother and father dolls down facing each other. Turns them back again when they will not stay in that position. Lays the dolls down on their backs, shifting them around as follows: *a*) #1 next to mother doll—back to back; *b*) #1 next to #3; *c*) mother doll next to father doll; *d*) #2 next to father doll; *e*) #3 next to mother doll and #1 next to #3. She follows the letters on the play box with her finger. JH again indicates the members of Naichó's family by means of gestures and lip movements. Naichó shifts #2 next to mother doll and stands father doll up where #2 had been. Manipulates arms of father doll. Puts #1 on shoulder of father doll. When it falls off she leaves it awhile and then replaces it. Kayolí adjusts one arm of father doll. Naichó places #1 next to #3. Puts #1 in father doll's arms as if in nursing position. Puts #1 next to #3. Lays father doll on top. The order of the dolls is now: father, #2, mother, #3, #1. Naichó places mother in sitting position. Puts father doll on all fours. Puts #3 between mother doll's legs *1*. Puts #2 between mother doll's legs *2*. Puts #1 on father doll's back. Nenarachí is present.[2] When Naichó puts mother doll on father doll's back *3*, she looks at Nenarachí, becomes confused, looks down, and removes mother doll. Takes #2 and #3 from between mother doll's legs and lays mother doll down. #1 has fallen off father

---

[1] Naichó is one of the cases discussed in Henry (6).
[2] She came in during the play but it is not clear at just what point.

doll's back and Naichó puts it back. She puts #2 and #3 together on the left side of mother doll. Puts father doll next to mother doll, the father doll on all fours. Puts #1 on father doll's back. Wetél is under a chair playing with a broken part of it. Naichó angrily calls examiner's attention to it. Kayolí says to Naichó: "Well, that's enough," but Naichó keeps on playing. Denikí takes #2 and Naichó hits him and takes away the doll. Denikí scratches her and she gives back the doll. She puts #3 next to mother doll. Puts #1 to nurse at mother doll's breast. Takes #1 from mother doll and puts it on father doll's back. Examiner terminates play.

Trial II. Same day. Puts #1 on father doll. Puts #2 on father doll and #1 in mother doll's arms. Puts #1 to nurse at mother doll's breast. Puts father doll on mother doll in position of intercourse *1* and places the genitals in contact.

Trial III. 10–13–37. Picks up turtle and lays it down. Lays dolls in a row. Picks up turtle and drops it. Picks up #1 doll. Sets it down and picks up mother doll. Sets down mother doll and picks up #1 doll. Puts it on and between the outspread thighs of the mother doll *1*. Puts #1 doll on mother doll's head. Stands up father doll. Picks up #1 doll and sets it on father doll's shoulders. Father doll and #1 doll fall. She sets them up again. Takes #1 doll off father doll and puts father doll's arms up so that they meet in a circle above its head. Plays with father doll, moving the limbs and showing it to examiner. Plays with father doll's penis for awhile and makes a good one. Sets up father doll again and smiles happily. After a short interruption she puts #1 doll to nurse at mother doll's breast.

Trial IV. 10–29–37. Puts ear-shaped pieces of clay over the ears of the dolls. Picks up #1 doll and looks at its ears. Seems perplexed. Puts breasts on #1 doll. Puts father doll on mother doll in position of intercourse *1*. Leaves father doll on mother doll and makes ears on #1 doll. Puts penis on #1 doll. Puts #1 doll on #2 doll in copulating position *2*. Takes great care that penis enter #2 doll. Lays mother and father dolls on their sides facing each other. Carefully places penis of father doll in vagina of mother doll *3*. When the dolls fall over Naichó screams: "*Way!*" Puts mother doll on its side and tries to keep father doll beside it in position of intercourse *4*. The doll will not stay. Puts mother doll on its back with its arms out holding the father doll on top of it in position of intercourse *5*. Puts father doll's arm around mother doll and seems very pleased. Kayolí, Dañakána, Simíti, and Yatákana start to box. Naichó fills the hands of the #2 doll with clay. Does the same with #1 doll. The girls continue to box. Naichó puts clay at bottom of #1 doll's feet. The girls yell at Naichó to stop playing and let Yatákana play. Naichó plays a little longer and then motions to examiner. She stops.

Trial V. 11–5–37. *Note:* Since Naichó is motherless no mother doll was included in this experiment. When the dolls were presented to Naichó the doll that had been the mother doll in the previous experiments was called Yalákachitn (#3), the doll that had been Yalákachitn in the previous experiments was called Nenarachí (#2), and the doll that had been Nenarachí in the previous experiments was called Naichó (#1).

Picks up scissors. Bubbles saliva between her lips. Puts down scissors. Puts vulva on #1 doll. Places #2 doll near father doll. Puts vulva on #2 doll. Puts breasts on father doll although it still has penis and testicles from a preceding experiment. Shows examiner the breasts she has put on father doll. Looks at father doll for awhile. Puts down father doll. Picks up scissors and makes a threatening gesture to Kapíetn who is looking in at the door. Places the material in a row as follows: scissors, father doll, #2 doll, #1 doll, #3 doll. Pays no attention at all to the #3 doll. It is the only doll that has neither genitals nor breasts. Puts breasts on #1 doll and shows them to examiner. Picks up #2 doll, makes breasts, puts them on. Naichó's father comes to the door and talks for awhile. She does not look up at him at all. Naichó puts breasts and vulva on #3 doll. She looks at the breasts a long time. Puts lump of clay over mouth of #3 doll completely covering it. Looks at it awhile and then removes it. Makes little blobs of clay and puts one over each nail on the play box. They project slightly above the surface of the box on which she is playing. Takes the clay off the nails and makes one round lump of it. Sits a long time watching the examiner write. Lawésaka-chiyi comes to the door. Examiner asks Naichó whether she wants to stop. Naichó says: "No." Examiner asks her whether she wants to stay and Naichó, very much embarrassed, says something that sounds like "I'll stay here." She smiles, walks to wall of house, breaks off a piece of the cane. Makes a clay fish and spits it on the cane. Does the same with another clay fish. Puts them down and picks up a candle that is lying on the box. Scratches off bits of wax with her finger nail. Puts the candle next to the #3 doll. Sits up #3 doll. Sits it on her own lap. Removes vulva and breasts. Tries to make doll sit and when she does not succeed indicates that examiner make the doll sit. Examiner does so. Naichó picks up #2 doll, removes the vulva and breasts and puts the doll down. Removes the vulva and breasts from #1 doll. Picks up father doll and removes breasts. Looks at it awhile. Holds the doll up questioningly. Examiner says: "Yes," and Naichó removes penis and testicles. Makes a ball of all the clay and impales it on a piece of cane about two feet long. Tries to push the cane into the ground like a fish spit, but then removes the clay and throws the cane away. Puts down clay. Picks up father doll, turns it upside down in leapfrog position. Picks it up again and turns the head around completely to the back. Turns the hands around to the back. Turns the head and hands back to normal position. Lays father doll on own lap. Picks up #3 doll and is about to place it on the father doll. Looks at it again. Puts large vulva on #3 doll and lays the doll on the box. Puts a penis on the father doll and puts father doll on #3 doll *1*. Sees examiner watching and removes father doll. Examiner smiles and continues writing, pretending not to look at Naichó. Naichó replaces father doll on #3 doll *2*. Picks up father doll in one hand and #3 doll in the other, carefully inserts penis into vagina *3*, and shows it to examiner. Lays them both down on the box, father doll on top of #3 doll. Again picks up father doll and lays it on #3 doll *4*, its penis touching the anal region. Sits looking at them. Puts #3 doll on top of father doll, the penis of the father doll in the anal region of the mother doll *5*. Looks at dolls. Cuts a small piece of paper she finds on the floor with the scissors. Cuts it into tiny pieces. Cuts the lump of clay. Puts one of the pieces she has cut off on the neck of the #2 doll. It falls off. Again she cuts paper into tiny pieces. Seems bored. Picks up a long piece of cane and breaks off a piece. Throws it away. Cuts up another tiny piece of paper. Stretches. Picks up piece of paper half an inch square and cuts it up. #3 doll and father doll are still in the previous position. Naichó looks around for things to cut, opening and closing the scissors. Finds nothing but the tiny pieces of paper she has already cut up. Puts scissors down. Takes father doll and improves penis. Puts father doll next to #3 doll, penis in contact with vulva *6*. The dolls are lying on their sides facing each other. Naichó picks up #3 doll and puts it on her own lap. Turns the doll face down and puts clay on the region where the anus would be. Puts a hole in the center. Shows it to examiner. Puts the father doll down on its back with the #3 doll on top of it *7*, also on its back. The penis of the father doll is in the "anus" of the #3 doll. The penis falls off. Naichó removes the vulva and the "anus" from the #3 doll. Picks up scissors and puts them down. Puts #3 doll and father doll side by side in copulating position *8*. Pushes them close together. Neither has genitals now. Puts #3 doll on top of father doll *9*. Puts #1 doll beside them. Puts #2 doll beside #1 doll. She just sits there. Examiner sends her home after she sits a long time doing nothing—but hating to give up the dolls.

Pattern of Hostility
    Doubtful
Pattern of Sexual Objects
    Direction
        1. #2-mother, #3-mother, mother-father
        2. father-mother
        3. #1-mother
        4. father-mother, #1-#2, father-mother (3 times)
        5. father-#3 (9 times)
    Forms
    Father-mother: 1) puts mother doll on back of father doll; 2) puts dolls
        in position of intercourse, genitals in contact.
    Father-#1:
    Father-#2:
    Father-#3: 1) puts father doll on #3 doll; 2) carefully inserts penis of
        father doll into vagina of #3 doll; 3) has penis of father doll touch anal
        region of #3 doll.
    Mother-#1: 1) places #1 between thighs of mother doll.
    Mother-#2: 1) places #2 between legs of mother doll.
    Mother-#3: 1) places #3 between legs of mother doll.
    #1-#2: 1) places #1 on #2 after putting a penis on #1.

Other Patterns

Regression: frequently puts #1 doll to nurse at breast of mother doll, and also places at the breast of father doll.

TAPÁÑI

Age: 8–9
Sex: female
Siblings: Yorodaikolík, male, age 4
Denikí, male, age 15 months

Trial I. 6–24–37. At first Tapáñi pays no attention to the dolls, only playing with the turtle. Then she picks up self doll and places it on mother doll's arms. Simíti puts the two other dolls on mother doll's shoulder. Tapáñi growls at her. Tapáñi plays with turtle. It goes toward self doll but does not strike it. Examiner says: "Perhaps it likes you and so it won't bite you. But perhaps it will bite anyone it doesn't like." Tapáñi says "Yes." She then makes the turtle bite mother doll (1) and both sibling dolls (2) (3), and says "It doesn't like them so it bites them. It doesn't bite Simíti and Dañakána because it likes them." She has turtle bite mother doll and both sibling dolls over and over again (4) (5) (6). Then she puts turtle near self doll. Examiner: "Has it bitten you?" Tapáñi: "No. Look, it likes me."

Trial II. Afternoon of same day. Puts baby doll at mother doll's breast. Yorodaikolík is present. He bends down, puts his face close to the mother doll's breast, and makes believe he is nursing. Tapáñi puts Yorodaikolík doll to nurse at mother doll's breast, but it falls through the arms of the mother doll because the space is too large. Tapáñi puts self doll there and fixes the arms so that they will hold her. She has put the face of the self doll right at the breast of the mother doll.

Trial III. 6-25-37. Immediately puts self doll to nurse, and places arms of mother doll very tenderly around self doll. Leaves self doll at mother doll's breast and ignores sibling dolls. Blows bubbles on bubble pipe while dolls are in this position. Examiner: "Perhaps Yorodaikolík would like to nurse." Tapáñi takes self doll away and puts Yorodaikolík doll to nurse. Stands self doll next to mother doll. Puts self doll in her own lap and covers it with her own dress. Lifts mother doll (1) and acts as if it were about to strike examiner (2). Throws Yorodaikolík doll to one side (3) and puts baby doll to nurse. Tapáñi is distracted here by Naichó who is playing with a mechanical mouse and with a mechanical tank. Then Tapáñi takes baby doll away from mother doll (4) and puts self doll to nurse. Picks up self doll and mother doll, keeping them in the same position and starts to keen. She keens with her mother's keening song. Tapáñi keens a long time and then puts baby doll to nurse holding mother doll and baby doll in her hands. Her mother calls her and Tapáñi shouts back: "What?" When no answer comes from the mother Tapáñi remains where she is. She puts down mother doll and baby doll (5), then picks up mother doll and puts self doll to nurse again, keening all the time. Naichó watches Tapáñi and Tapáñi growls at her.

Trial IV. 6–27–37. Yorodaikolík makes a violent gesture with his fist toward the Tapáñi doll. She says "Stop it!" He repeats it looking at her. When examiner puts the Yorodaikolík doll to the breast of mother doll Tapáñi asks to have the mechanical mouse go. An interruption occurs in which other children manipulate the material. Then Tapáñi puts the Yorodaikolík doll to breast of mother doll. When JH says: "It is Yorodaikolík" Tapáñi takes it away and puts the baby doll in its place but places the Yorodaikolík doll very carefully at the other breast of the mother doll. Tapáñi knocks down the mother doll twice (1) with the father doll[3] (2). She says of the father doll, "My father, more's the pity" (3). Tapáñi and Yorodaikolík now struggle for a blanket. Tapáñi wants it all for herself. At last she hits Yorodaikolík on the cheek with her fist and he goes home weeping.

Trial V. 10–10–37. Tapáñi puts baby doll to breast of mother doll. Says to examiner, "When you go home I'll go with you so that I can eat white people's food." At this point Wetél comes into the house with a ball of cooked wild fruit in his hand. Tapáñi says "Why don't you share your food with me? Because you're stingy." She cannot concentrate on the dolls because of Wetél's food, and also because our cook is cooking a duck. Tapáñi asks for the turtle, and has it bite all the dolls (1) (2) (3) (4) (5). However, she directs it particularly toward the mother doll and the Yorodaikolík doll. Examiner: "Why does it bite you?" Tapáñi: "Because it does not like me." Turtle now bites father (6), self (7), mother (8). Tapáñi puts turtle on top of baby doll and it bites (9). Puts turtle on self doll and it bites (10). Directs turtle so that it bites mother doll (11). Puts turtle on own real thigh (12) and says: "It's biting me." Puts turtle on all the dolls one after the other and says: "It's biting them" (13) (14) (15) (16) (17).

Trial VI. 10–14–37. Picks up self doll. Lifts her own blouse and says "Look at my breasts." Points to self doll and says "It has none." Mátakana is on JH's lap. Tapáñi says to her "I'll have intercourse with you." Repeats. Yorodaikolík is now on JH's lap. Mátakana says "He wants to nurse." Tapáñi puts tremendous breasts on self doll, and also repairs breasts of mother doll. Yorodaikolík points to his breasts and says: "My breasts." Mátakana again says to Yorodaikolík, "He wants to nurse." Tapáñi picks up Yorodaikolík doll and asks whether it is Denikí. Examiner says "No," and points to baby doll. Tapáñi drops Yorodaikolík doll, picks up baby doll, and puts it to nurse at breast of mother doll, saying "Nurse." Places Yorodaikolík doll next to self doll, beside baby doll. Yorodaikolík punches Tapáñi on the head. She raises her hand in a threatening gesture. Yorodaikolík raises his hand again glowering at her, and then runs away. All the children run to our rice pot. Tapáñi comes back, picks up self doll, and says: "I'm a cute and beautiful little thing."

Trial VII. 10–15–37. Says: "Shall I make a vulva? Oh, there is one." Puts baby doll to nurse, its mouth to breast of mother doll. Puts self doll next to baby doll and brother doll on the other side. Puts brother doll on the same side and self doll

---

[3] Although the father has been dead about six months, a father doll was included in this and the following experiment in order to study the attitude of Tapáñi toward her father.

farther away. Bites self doll with turtle (1). Turtle now bites mother (2), self (3), baby (4), brother (5). The turtle goes on the baby doll (6). Turtle bites self doll 5 times (7). Turtle goes toward genital of self doll (8). Turtle bites mother doll (9). Tapáñi changes baby doll to other side of mother doll. Makes the mother doll hold the baby doll well with both arms. Puts brother doll on other arm, self doll on the outside. Turtle bites self doll over and over again (10), but there is no room for the turtle on the mother doll's side. Self doll falls down, and Maralú, who has been saying "I'm next," says "Dead." Tapáñi definitely directs turtle to bite self doll again and again (11). Turtle bites mother doll (12) and self doll (13). Tapáñi again directs turtle to bite mother doll (14) and self doll (15) with the dolls in a different position.

Trial VIII. 10-29-37. Puts tremendous penis on brother doll. Makes penis for baby doll and says "Denikí." This penis is also large but not as well made or as clearly defined. She asks whether she should make a vulva for self doll; "Shall I make its vulva?" Puts large vulva on self doll. Asks who the mother doll is. Examiner says "Diwá'i,"[4] and Tapáñi says "Ts, ts, why of course!" Tapáñi looks at mother doll for some time. Lays it down and asks "Shall I make breasts for it?" Examiner: "Yes." Tapáñi puts vulva on mother doll and says "Look, there is no more clay." There was plenty of clay for everything but she has made very large organs on all the dolls. She points to mother doll and says "Look, no breasts." Examiner tells her that if she wishes she may take some clay off some of the organs she has already made and make some breasts. Tapáñi does so. She turns mother doll's head round and round. Puts baby doll beside mother doll—not nursing. Puts brother doll next to baby doll, and then self doll next to brother doll.

Trial IX. 11-3-37. When given mother doll she improves the appearance of the breasts. Then she picks up self doll and is on the point of putting herself at mother doll's breast. Changes her mind and picks up baby doll and puts him to nurse at mother doll's breast.

Pattern of Hostility

Direction

1. mother, both siblings, mother and both siblings repeatedly
3. mother, brother, baby
4. mother (twice), father (twice)
5. father, self, mother, baby, brother, father, self, mother, baby, self, mother, self, all
7. self, mother, self, baby, brother, baby, self (6 times), self, mother, self (repeatedly); self, mother, self, mother, self

Forms

Baby: 1) turtle bites; 2) removes from breast.

Mother: 1) turtle bites; 2) acts is if mother doll were about to strike examiner; 3) knocks down with father doll.

---

4 Her mother's name.

Father: 1) uses the doll to knock down the mother doll; 2) (verbal) "My father, more's the pity."

Brother: 1) turtle bites; 2) throws to one side.

Self: 1) turtle bites; 2) (verbal) "It doesn't like me"; 3) places turtle on own real thigh and says: "It's biting me."

Restitution

of baby: restores baby to mother.

Pattern of Sexual Objects

None

Other Patterns

Regression: frequently puts self to nurse.

YORODAIKOLÍK

Age: 4
Sex: male
Siblings: Tapáñi, female, age 8–9
Denikí, male, age 15 months

Trial I. 6–24–37. He bends down and makes believe he is nursing. Puts his face close to breast of mother doll.

Trial II. 6–25–37. Places sister doll and self doll to nurse. Ignores brother doll. Tires of play in a very short time.

Trial III. 6–27–37. Makes violent gesture with fist toward sister doll (1). She says "Stop it!" He repeats it (2), looking at her. He makes a sucking noise over head of mother doll. Makes a violent gesture toward the mother doll (3). When Simíti puts the Yorodaikolík doll between the legs of the mother doll, Yorodaikolík says "Intercourse" *1*. He again puts self doll between legs of mother doll *2* and says they are having intercourse.

Trial IV. 10–2–37. Darotoyí puts Tapáñi doll on Yorodaikolík doll. Yorodaikolík says "She's deflowered" *1* (1). He puts self doll on top of sister doll *2*. Lapse of several minutes while other children manipulate the material. The last move is made by Darotoyí who has the turtle bite the mother doll and the baby doll. Yorodaikolík has the turtle bite the self doll over and over again (2). Has turtle bite mother doll (3). Directs turtle to bite sister doll but it bites Denikí doll because Yorodaikolík does not control the turtle properly. He says: "It bit my sister" (4). Directs turtle to sister doll (5). Puts away the sister doll (6), then the mother doll (7), and then the Denikí doll (8), saying: "They are far away." Leaves only the self doll. Turtle bites self doll over and over again (9). [Lapse of several minutes during which the following things occur in order: Yorodaikolík and Darotoyí hesitate between going and remaining; Darotoyí manipulates the material; the last thing he does is have the turtle swallow the penis of a doll representing his own older brother; Yorodaikolík and Darotoyí hesitate between going and remaining.] Then Yorodaikolík puts sister doll next to his own real penis *3*. Puts self doll on sister doll *4*.

Trial V. 10–9–37. Tanorow'í is playing with the dolls. Yorodaikolík and Darotoyí have just had a quarrel outside the house. Yorodaikolík comes in and says that Darotoyí is a thief. Yorodaikolík takes the doll that has represented himself in previous experiments and says "I'll kill him." He demonstrateș how he is going to cut off the head. Says: "I'll take its shirt off." Puts self doll down on its back and places the mother doll on top of it. Says: "Intercourse." Tanorow'í takes the doll away. When Yorodaikolík gets the doll back he puts the self doll on top of the mother doll and places the penis of the self doll carefully in the vagina of the mother doll.

Trial VI. 10–14–37. Puts brother doll under mother doll face up and says "Intercourse" *1*. Puts self doll and sister doll on mother doll's back. Picks up knife[5] and sister doll and passes knife over sister doll's throat (1), saying "I kill her." Then he passes the knife over her feet (2). Says: "I kill her vulva," and passes the knife over vulva of sister doll (3). Says: "Her belly," and does the same on belly of sister doll (4). Picks up self doll and repeats the movement on the throat and penis of the self doll (5), saying "I cut off my penis." Mátakana takes away her knife. Yorodaikolík puts brother doll on mother doll, the penis carefully in the vagina *2*, saying "Yichína."[6] Puts brother doll to mother doll's mouth, then to breast of mother doll. Holds on to mother doll. Puts self doll next to sister doll. Puts down mother doll and holds brother doll. Puts brother doll to breast of mother doll and says "I'll stop."

Trial VII. 10–14–37. Yorodaikolík replaces Mátakana who is still standing near. Yorodaikolík carefully screws a screw into the eye of father doll. Seizes mother doll, saying "My mother." Gives the doll to examiner, saying "My sister." Insists on giving it to examiner. Calls it Nenarachí. When Mátakana touches the mother doll Yorodaikolík pokes her in the eye. He says "I'll stop now," and walks away saying "I'm angry now." He makes a game of it; walks back and forth, saying "I'm angry. I'll come back."

Trial VIII. 10–15–37. Puts self doll between legs of mother doll *1*. Tries hard and at last succeeds in having turtle bite sister doll (1). Turtle bites sister doll again and knocks it off the play table (2). Turtle bites self doll (3). Puts self doll on the other side of mother doll so that turtle can bite self doll (4). Turtle bites sister doll repeatedly (5). Turtle bites self doll repeatedly (6). JH: "Why are you bitten?" Yorodaikolík: "Because I am sick."

Trial IX. 10–29–37. Puts mother doll face down on top of all the dolls and says "Look! She is having intercourse" *1*. Lays mother doll down on its back and places self doll on top of mother doll in copulating position *2*. Places brother doll on sister doll in copulating position *3*. Puts baby doll on top of mother doll, and says "He has intercourse" *4*. Puts self doll on top of sister doll *5*, and says "Has intercourse."

[5] The knife had been left there by a child.

[6] His brother's other name.

Trial X. 10–30–37. Makes penis for self doll. Puts vulva on sister doll and penis on brother doll. Looks at mother doll and says "No vulva." Puts vulva on mother doll. It is not as well made as the one he made for the sister doll, even though the one on the sister doll is smaller. Mother doll's genital looks like this ⬭; while sister doll's vulva looks like this ◑. The center marks are made with finger nail. He makes no breasts for mother doll until examiner remarks that there are no breasts. Then Yorodaikolík puts breasts on mother doll.

Trial XI. 11–1–37. Places dolls in following position: mother, self, brother, sister. Picks up scissors and says "I know how." Puts scissors down and tells examiner that Denikí has *álik*.[7] Covers all the dolls with his own skirt. Uncovers them, picks up mother doll and puts it down. Picks up sister doll and tries to make it stand. When it falls he says "It died, look." He does this over and over again, and says "It fell on top of me." He puts self doll in position of intercourse with sister doll *1* and frantically begins piling all the dolls on top of one another, the mother doll on top of all *2*. Puts scissors on top of all of them and says "A heap." Says: "Look, I have intercourse," and puts self doll on top of sister doll; then brother doll *4*, and mother doll on top of all *5*. Puts scissors across self doll and sister doll and says of the scissors, "It has teeth." Goes to side of house and says he will close up the hole made in the wall by the children. He wants to do this so that the other children will not be able to look in. Says: "I am going home. It's evening." Goes to door, bends down to ground and calls "Mother!"[8] When he gets no answer he says to examiner, "I'm not going." He walks around a few moments and then says "I'm going home." He goes.

Trial XII. 11–3–37. Points to sister doll and says "This one has no genital." Makes a very big one. Says: "Suña, Tapáñi says she has a big vulva" (1). He shows it to the examiner. Yorodaikolík remarks that self doll has no penis. Says: "Look, I know how to make a penis." Puts penis on self doll. Squashes it (2). Scratches it (3) and says "The penis' opening." Says it looks like a vulva. Does the same to brother doll (4). Puts a new vulva on mother doll. Puts breasts on brother doll, and says that he's putting breasts on Denikí. Puts small blob of clay into vagina of sister doll, saying "The vagina's clitoris." Puts tiny breasts on sister doll and closes its eyes with clay (5). Says: "The covering of its eyes. *O way!* Blind!" He makes the abdomen, a clay blob on the abdomen. Says: "*O way!* Blind!" Asks for father doll. Picks up scissors. Lays them down. Picks up sister doll and says "*O way!*" Self doll and brother doll are side by side. Lays sister doll next to self doll, then brother doll, then mother doll. Pushes scissors closer to mother doll. Puts clay on head of sister doll and calls it "its hair." Puts extra nipple on mother doll's breast. Removes it and puts it on brother doll's head, calling it a hat. Handles scissors again. Asks for bubble pipe. Says he's thirsty. Drinks. Asks for hockey ball[9] and immediately puts it on mother doll's head (6). Picks up sister doll and puts hockey ball beside mother. Places sister doll beside

[7] A food made from cooked forest fruit.
[8] Really "my widowed mother."
[9] A very heavy wooden ball about an inch and a half in diameter.

mother doll. Places brother doll beside mother doll. Then places brother doll beside sister doll, self doll next to brother doll, then scissors. Treats the scissors like
a doll. Pushes metal object into mother doll's foot (7). Picks up hockey ball.
Yatákana looks in and Yorodaikolík puts down hockey ball. He puts sister doll
on genital of mother doll *1*, then across neck of mother doll. Puts brother doll on
top of sister doll *2*, self on top of all *3* and says "A heap." In answer to examiner's
question, "Why is there a heap?" Yorodaikolík says "They are having intercourse." Yorodaikolík again puts sister doll across the breasts of the mother doll.
Places self on sister doll *4*, and brother doll on top of all *5*. Changes brother doll to
position on top of sister doll *6*. Then takes away self and brother dolls. Puts head
of self doll into cup of water and says "I'm bathing." Puts legs of self doll into
cup. Repeats. Puts self doll and brother doll (8) completely into cup. Takes out
brother doll and says: "Deniki drowned (9). I, on the other hand, did not drown."
Picks up scissors, looks angrily at Naichó at door, holds scissors up and puts them
down again. Picks up hockey ball and rolls it on mother doll's face (10). Makes
shoes for mother doll. Stands sister doll on head. Takes shoes off mother doll's
feet and puts them on sister doll's head, saying "The hat's brim." Puts sister doll
aside on toy box within reach. Pulls up sleeves of self doll, drinks the water in
which he had bathed the two dolls, and says "I'll stop now."

Pattern of Hostility
  Direction
    3. sister (twice), mother.
    4. sister, self, mother, sister (3 times), mother, brother, self
    5. uncertain
    6. sister (4 times), self (twice)
    7. father, sister
    8. sister (twice), self (twice), sister (repeatedly), self (repeatedly)
    11. sister, self, sister and self
    12. sister, self (4 times), brother, sister (twice), mother (twice), brother
        (twice), mother
  Forms
    Brother: 1) (verbal) "They are far away"; 2) squashes penis; 3) puts doll in
      cup of water; 4) (verbal) "Deniki drowned."
    Mother: 1) shakes fist at mother doll; 2) turtle bites; 3) (verbal) "They are
      far away"; 4) gives it away; 5) denies its identity (i.e., calls it Nenarachí);
      6) puts ball on head; 7) pushes metal object into foot; 8) rolls ball on face.
    Sister: 1) shakes fist at sister doll; 2) (verbal) "She is deflowered"; 3) (verbal)
      "It bit my sister"; 4) turtle bites; 5) (verbal) "They are far away"; 6)
      passes knife across throat; 7) (verbal) "I kill her"; 8) passes knife over feet
      and vagina; 9) (verbal "I kill her vagina"; 10) passes knife over abdomen;
      11) (verbal) "Her belly"; 12) (verbal) "It died"; 13) (verbal) "My sister
      says she has a big vagina"; 14) covers eyes with clay; 15) "*O way!* Blind!"

Self: 1) turtle bites; 2) passes knife over throat and penis; 3) (verbal)
"I cut off my penis"; 4) (verbal) "I am sick"(?); 5) squashes penis; 6)
scratches penis.

Restitution
Brother: restoration of brother
Mother: makes shoes for mother doll.
Sister: makes hat (brim).

Pattern of Sexual Objects

Direction
3. mother-self
4. sister-self; self-sister; self-sister
5. mother-uncertain; mother-uncertain
6. mother-brother; brother-mother
8. self-mother
9. mother-all; self-mother; brother-sister; brother-mother; self-sister
11. self-sister; (piling) mother-all; self-sister; (piling) brother and self on
sister; mother-all
12. (piling) sister-mother, brother-sister, self-all; (piling) sister-mother (?),
self-sister, brother-all; brother-sister

Forms
Mother-self: 1) (verbal) "Intercourse"; 2) self between legs of mother;
3) (verbal) "They are having intercourse"; 4) self on mother.
Sister-self: 1) (verbal) "She is deflowered"; 2) self on sister; 3) sister next to
his own real penis; 4) (verbal) "Has intercourse"; 5) self and brother on
sister.
Mother-brother: 1) brother under mother; 2) (verbal) "Intercourse"; 3)
brother on mother.
Sister-brother: 1) brother on sister.
Sister-mother: 1) puts sister on vulva of mother.

Other Patterns

Regression: pretends to nurse at breast of mother doll; makes sucking noises
above mother doll; places self doll to nurse.
Feature: spread of sexuality.

DENIKÍ

Age: 15 months
Sex: male
Siblings: Tapáñi, female, age 8–9
Yorodaikolík, male, age 4

Trial I. 10–11–37. [The dolls are in the condition they were in at the end of the
preceding experiment. There is a mother doll that has genitals and breasts; and a
father doll that has a penis. There are three smaller dolls with vulvas but no

breasts. In the present experiment the small dolls are numbered 1, 2, and 3 respectively in order of size. They are not named.]

Naichó puts #1 doll on father doll's lap. Deniki puts #3 on #1 and then #2 on top. Takes off all dolls. Puts #1 doll on top of father doll's head repeatedly. Picks up #3 doll and turns it around. Stands it on its head. Piles all dolls on father doll. Takes them off. Gives #1 to JH. Gives #3 to JH. Gives #2 to examiner. Takes back all dolls. Again piles dolls #1, #2, and #3 on father doll's legs. Takes them off. Does it again. Continues piling. Examiner puts #1 doll to nurse. Deniki takes it away and puts #3 there instead. Piles the dolls again. When he drops the father doll Nenarachi yells: "Stop it!" three times and slaps Deniki. He looks at her a long time and then starts to cry.

Trial II. 10–29–37. [In this and the following experiments the dolls are named as usual.] Deniki holds mother doll and self doll all the time. Puts down mother doll. Shows self doll to examiner and examiner calls it Deniki. Picks up mother doll again and holds on to both. Puts down mother doll and self doll on top of it, face down, legs on breasts of mother doll. He crows with delight. Tries to put self doll in nursing position; it falls down. Picks up sister doll which has a breast on it and gives self doll to Naichó. Examiner removes breast from sister doll and Deniki looks at examiner perplexed. Deniki takes self doll from Naichó. Picks up sister doll and fingers place where breast was. Gives sister doll to Naichó. Picks up mother doll and puts sister doll next to it. Gives self doll and then sister doll to Naichó. Takes them back again and puts sister doll next to mother doll. Gives three dolls to Naichó and takes back mother doll. Takes them all back. Lays mother doll down on its back. Piles three smaller dolls one on top of the other. Lays sister doll against legs of mother doll. Piles other dolls on top of sister doll. Picks up mother doll and lays it on top of smaller dolls. Gives brother doll to Naichó and takes it back. Gives self doll to Naichó and takes it back. Lays down sister doll and piles others on top with mother doll on top of all. He crows with delight. Gives all the dolls to Naichó and takes them back. Puts brother doll on top of sister doll. Naichó is putting clay ears on dolls. Deniki takes dolls away from Naichó. He puts down all the dolls and picks up mother doll and puts it down. Puts sister doll on its side and self doll beside it. Puts mother doll beyond and other dolls next to it. Changes the positions. Again puts down mother doll, but closer to self doll this time. Makes self doll sit up and he crows. Tries to make sister doll stand but it falls. He says "*U u gau*."[10] Looks at mother doll closely and smiles. Picks up sister doll and looks closely. Picks up all the dolls and goes toward door. At the door Dañakána motions him to go back. He brings back the dolls and again moves toward the door. Dañakána blocks his passage and Deniki comes back. He picks up mother doll and stands it on its head. Lays it down. Picks up sister doll. Examiner says: "Tapáñi" and Deniki throws down the doll. He picks up mother doll and self doll. Examiner says: "Deniki" and points to self doll. Deniki puts self doll to breast of mother doll.

[10] Baby-talk for *pumagá*, it fell down.

He puts down all the dolls. Puts self doll and then sister doll on mother doll. Mother doll is lying on its back, self doll is lying on it face down. Deniki crows delightedly. He picks up sister doll and puts his finger on the vulva. Picks up mother doll and touches breasts. Picks up sister doll and tries to separate legs. They don't move. Puts it down. Picks up self doll and touches its back. Moves the celluloid in and out with his fingers. Naichó has been shaking a tin rattle. It falls out of her hands and strikes sister doll, shattering it. Only the head remains whole. Deniki picks up the head and looks at it. He stands the mother doll on top of the head, inside the neck. He leaves.

Trial III. 10–30–37. Deniki comes in with his mother. Hands his mother the mother doll and takes it back. Takes self doll from his mother. Gives sister and self dolls to his mother. Takes them both back. His mother takes his sister doll. Deniki takes it back. He gives sister doll, self doll, and mother doll to his mother. Takes them back. Lays down all the dolls. Gives examiner sister doll and hands self doll to his mother. Takes them all back and lays them down. Indicates desire for clay. Puts clay on top of the penis of the baby doll. It falls off. Gives examiner the clay. Asks for it again. Examiner puts penis on baby and brother dolls, and vulvas on mother and sister dolls, and gives them to Deniki. He takes a piece of clay off the mother doll's breast. His mother leaves. Deniki takes piece of clay off sister doll's vulva. Lays mother doll on top of all the dolls. Lawésakachiyi repairs breast of mother doll. When Lawésakachiyi wants to pick up another doll Deniki brandishes a doll in his hand as though to strike him. All the boys leave the house after frantically calling the examiner to look at their [invisible] hurts. Deniki takes pieces off genitals of each doll. Removes penis of self doll. It was very loosely put on. Deniki stands sister doll on head after examiner calls it by name. Deniki sits brother doll down and sits down self doll. Tries to stand sister doll up. It falls and he puts it on top of self doll. Both dolls are face down. He hears dogs barking. He gives all dolls to examiner and goes out but comes back in a minute. His brother comes in. Deniki is in the act of putting all the dolls under the cardboard which is being used as play table. Dañakána comes to look in at the crack in the side of the house. Deniki raises his arm threateningly and points her out to examiner. He points exactly as the older children do when they point out another child doing something they think we'll disapprove of. Deniki gives examiner sister, brother, and self dolls, but keeps the mother doll. Takes all back. Puts self doll on top of mother doll. Mother doll is lying on its back, the self doll lies across breast and shoulder of mother doll. Deniki piles other dolls on top of mother doll. They all fall over. Deniki picks up self doll and says *"Kakák."*[11] Picks up sister doll in one hand and self doll in other. Makes move to throw away sister doll but doesn't. Gives examiner mother doll and picks up other dolls. Puts them on a chair. Takes back mother doll and gives examiner the sister doll. Examiner calls it by name. Deniki takes back sister doll. His brother takes possession of all the dolls and Deniki starts to cry. The brother stops and gives the dolls to Deniki

[11] Baby talk for *wakák*, broken.

who stops crying. Brother takes two child dolls and tells examiner to hide them. Examiner gives all the dolls to Denikí. Denikí picks up mother doll in one hand, putting all the child dolls together. He stops to urinate, stepping back from the chair, urine running down his legs and on his feet. Comes back to chair, removes penis of brother doll. Brother says: "I'm going home," and Denikí quietly gives examiner all the dolls and follows his brother out.

Trial IV. 10–31–37. When examiner gives Denikí the sister doll Denikí immediately gives it to Yatákana and then takes it back. Denikí stands sister doll on its head, then tries to make it walk, holding it in his hand all the time. With the other hand he removes one breast of mother doll. Removes breasts of sister doll. Removes penis of self doll. Picks up sister doll and puts it down. Picks up mother doll and shows it to examiner. Examiner says "Diwá'i." Denikí attempts to repeat the name. He stands the mother doll on its head and points it out to examiner. Lays it down. Removes remaining breast of mother doll. Picks up brother doll, removes penis, and laughs. He always puts the clay on the box he is using as a table. Sits down self doll. Begins picking off the various pieces of clay. Puts them down again. Puts self doll face down in position for leap-frog game. Puts mother doll over the back of self doll and laughs. Does it twice more. Watches Naichó and Yatákana dancing and cries out to them: "Ho ho!" Picks up self doll and puts it to his face and crows delightedly. Picks up mother doll and sister doll and holds one in each hand. Puts mother doll near his own penis *1*. The girls have gone out. Yatákana comes back. Denikí gets up and strikes her. Examiner tells her to go out and Denikí comes back to his box laughing. Picks up scissors and makes cutting movement on sister doll's legs and head (1) and on mother doll's head (2). Gives brother doll to examiner. Again tries to cut sister doll (3), then self doll (4). Tries to cut off legs and head of self doll. Again bangs on head of sister doll (5). Gives scissors to examiner. All this time examiner has been holding brother doll, and the brother doll is the only one Denikí does not attack. Denikí gives self doll and then sister doll to examiner and goes toward the door, holding the mother doll. Comes back, gives mother doll to examiner, and goes home.

Trial V. 11–1–37. Picks up scissors. Examiner repeats names of dolls. Denikí picks up self doll and then sister doll. Stands up sister doll. It falls down. Denikí still holds on to self doll. Puts his mouth on mouth of brother doll. Picks up sister doll and drops it. Picks up brother doll and drops it. Picks up mother doll, sets it on its head and puts it down. Makes sister doll walk. Picks up self doll, which has no penis, with other hand puts it beyond his own leg on the ground far away from the other dolls and leaves it there. Is still holding sister doll. Puts it down. Picks up mother doll and takes off parts of its breasts and says "Kakák." Points to self doll still lying where he had put it and again says "Kakák." Puts down mother doll, picks up scissors and looks at it awhile. Puts it down again. Picks up mother doll and says "Kak."[12] He again picks up mother doll and shows it to ex-

---

[12] Another form of *kakák*.

aminer. Picks up each doll in succession and examiner names them. Denikí repeats this procedure with all except self doll. He picks up self doll and puts it down. Picks up mother doll and says "*Kak*." Picks up sister doll and stands it up. It falls. Picks it up again and stands it on his own knee, then on ground. Picks up scissors, holding sister doll in his hand. Drops the scissors and sister doll and picks up self doll, saying "*Kakák*" three times. Gives dolls to examiner. Examiner puts penis on self doll. Denikí looks at it awhile and puts it down. Gives mother doll to examiner. Picks up other dolls and gives them to examiner. Picks up scissors, gives them to examiner and goes home.

Trial VI. 11–2–37. Picks up self and brother dolls. Puts head of self doll on penis of brother doll. Shows self doll to his brother who looks in, to JH who comes in, and to examiner. Puts down self doll. Stands up sister doll over and over again when it falls. When it falls, he says "*Kak*," and rights it again. It falls and he says "*Kak*." Shows standing sister doll to examiner. Picks it up and points out the vulva with his index finger on the vulva. Picks up mother doll and then sister doll. Puts down sister doll but holds on to mother doll. Puts down mother doll. Picks up sister doll and shows it to examiner. Puts it down face down. Picks up mother doll and puts it down. Picks up sister doll. Examiner calls names of dolls as Denikí picks them up. Denikí pulls out arm of sister doll over and over again (1), saying "*Kak*," each time. He's trying to pull arm off. Puts down sister doll. Picks up mother doll and pulls arm out once (2). Puts it down. Picks up sister doll and pulls out arm (3), each time saying "*Kak*" in great glee. Stands up sister doll and when it falls, says: "*Kak*." Again he tries pulling arm out (4) saying "*Kak*" each time. Puts mother doll on his lap, laying it down on its back. Holds it there awhile and plays the same game of pulling out the arm of the sister doll (5). Puts sister doll on mother doll. Puts sister doll back. Picks up self doll and puts it on mother doll's thigh on its back. Puts self doll back on box, and puts brother doll on mother doll's thigh. Puts it back on box immediately. Picks up sister doll, pulls arm (6), and says "*Kak*." He has been holding mother doll all the time on his real lap. Removes breasts of mother doll and puts it back on box. Puts pieces of clay on box and leaves them there. Picks up mother doll and removes more clay off breasts. Tries to remove its mouth but cannot. Puts mother doll down on his lap. Picks up self doll and holds it up for examiner to see for some time. Puts self on mother doll. Puts self back. Holds mother doll with one hand all the time. Picks up mother doll, shows it to examiner and says "*Kak*." Puts down all the dolls. Mother doll falls off the box. He says "*Kak*," and puts it back. Shows it to examiner and says "*A a*."[13] Yorodaikolík comes to look in at side of house. Denikí picks up candle and says "*Kak*." Candle falls out of his hand. He picks up sister doll in one hand and mother in the other. Dumps mother doll down on all dolls except sister doll which he picks up. He's trying very hard to pull the arm out (7). Picks up self doll which had fallen off box when he pushed candle. Removes penis of self doll. Puts it and the doll down on box. Removes

[13] In Denikí's vocabulary "*A a*" is used to call attention to something.

part of sister doll's vulva. Takes off more of sister doll's vulva. Picks up mother doll having put down sister doll. Shows it to examiner. Examiner calls it Diwá'i. Deniki picks up brother doll and shows it to examiner. Examiner calls it Yorodaikolík. Repeats. Deniki picks up self doll. Yorodaikolík comes to hole in house wall and Deniki picks up mother doll and holds it out to Yorodaikolík. Yorodaikolík goes away and Deniki puts mother doll down, saying "*Kak.*" Examiner is chasing bunches of little girls away. Anetolí remains at door. Deniki points to Anetolí. Deniki holds on to self doll. Gives it to examiner. Gives candle, sister doll, and brother doll to examiner and goes out. The house is surrounded by screaming girls trying to get in.

Deniki comes right back. Picks up candle. Examiner puts scissors on box. Deniki immediately picks them up and makes cutting movements on legs of self doll (8), then legs of mother doll (9), and head of brother doll (10). He walks away with the scissors in his mouth. Puts scissors down after walking around the room awhile. Puts mother doll on examiner's lap. Examiner lets it fall off. Deniki picks it up and says "*Kak.*" Puts it on box. Gives mother doll to examiner. Deniki gives examiner scissors, brother doll, self doll, sister doll. Goes to door and goes home.

Trial VII. 11–2–37. Deniki is pushed into our house by his mother. He picks up sister doll and holds mother doll. Puts mother doll aside on the scissors. Picks up mother doll after putting self doll and brother doll a distance away together. Picks up mother doll and puts it aside away from self and brother dolls. Picks up sister doll and says "*Kak.*" Pulls arm out over and over again (1), saying "*Kak.*" Puts it down. Picks up brother doll and puts it down. Picks up scissors and treats it like sister doll's arm—pulls it and says "*Kak.*" Puts scissors into his mouth. Looks at all dolls. Picks up self doll, then scissors, and starts to cut back of self doll (2). Makes cutting movements on head of sister doll (3), then on head of mother doll (4), then cuts breasts of mother doll (5) removing a little at a time. Sticks the pieces of the breasts on the end of the scissors. Cuts the pieces into smaller pieces (6). Puts self doll into his mouth. Holds self doll out to examiner who then says "Deniki." Deniki puts down self doll. Picks up sister doll and gives it to examiner. Gives examiner mother doll, scissors, brother doll, self doll. Goes home.

Pattern of Hostility
  Direction
    2. sister
    3. sister
    4. sister, mother, sister, self, sister
    6. sister, mother, sister (5 times), self, mother, brother
    7. sister, self, sister, mother (3 times)
  Forms
    Brother: 1) cutting movements

Mother: 1) cutting movements; 2) pulls out arm; 3) cuts breasts.

Sister: 1) throws down; 2) cutting movements; 3) bangs on head; 4) pulls out arm over and over again.

Self: 1) cutting movements

Pattern of Sexual Objects

Direction

4. mother

Forms

Mother-self: 1) puts mother doll next to his real penis.

LAWÉSAKACHIYI

Age: 6

Sex: male

Siblings: Ináratakaik,[14] male, age 30

Chikáchigi, male, age 21

Pakchítn, male, age 17

Nasáitn, male, age 14

Trial I. 10–31–37. Makes penis for father doll, Pakchítn doll, and self doll. Penis of self doll is the largest. The penises are well formed. Puts self doll next to mother doll, father doll on the other side of self doll. Then Pakchítn and Nasáitn. His mother comes and sits down behind him and delouses him. He sits there playing with two marbles.

Trial II. Same day. Says he wants to play again. Dañakána is also in the house. Examiner gives dolls to Lawésakachiyi. Dañakána points out father doll and says to Lawésakachiyi: "Your father." He says to her angrily: "Your father." When examiner corroborates Dañakána's statement and calls the amputation doll Lawésakachiyi's father, he gets up, says "I'm bored" and goes home.

Trial III. 11–1–37. Comes in and says he wants to play. Examiner gives him the dolls calling them by name. He sits awhile looking at the girls who are looking in, and at last says "I'm bored" and goes home.

Trial IV. 11–3–37. Examiner removes the vulva of one of the dolls which is now to represent Pakchítn. Lawésakachiyi says "Don't! That's its penis!" Examiner: "Shall I make his penis?" Lawésakachiyi: "Don't." Picks up father doll, raises one leg in the air and says "Lame." He ignores all the dolls except the father doll. Now he puts them in the following order: mother, father, Pakchítn, Nasáitn, self. The mother doll has only one breast. Examiner suggests that Lawésakachiyi make the other. Lawésakachiyi says "I don't know how." Examiner: "Shall I make it?" Lawésakachiyi: "Yes." Examiner does so and Lawésakachiyi says "Make it very smooth." Examiner makes the nipples stand out but rounds them. Lawésakachiyi says "Good." Examiner asks Lawésakachiyi whether he knows how to make the father's penis. He says "I'll try." He makes a

---

[14] Married and moved to another village.

long, well shaped penis. Puts mother and father dolls face to face, genitals touching *1*. When father doll's penis falls off Lawésakachiyi repairs it. Lays mother
doll on its back and the father doll on top *2*. Picks up mother doll and looks at
vulva. Removes father doll's penis and inserts it in mother doll's vagina *3*,
then puts father on top *4*. Removes father doll, replaces penis. Now holding one
doll in each hand he again tries to put the genitals of the two dolls together *5*.
When he succeeds he is visibly pleased. He separates the dolls laying three child
dolls between them. Sits looking at the dolls. Takes a tiny drink of water. He is
not thirsty because he just had a drink. Looks outside. Says "I'll stop. Again at
noon. I'm bored to death." Examiner tells him to go home and he does.

Pattern of Hostility
  Direction
    4. father
  Forms
    Mother:
    Father: 1) (verbal) "Lame"; 2) removes penis and inserts in vagina.
Pattern of Sexual Objects
  Direction
    4. father-mother (4 times)
  Forms
    Father-mother: 1) puts face to face on side with genitals touching; 2) places
      in ventral-ventral position; 3) removes penis and inserts in vagina; 4)
      holding one in each hand puts genitals in contact.

SIMÍTI

Age: 10
Sex: female
Sibling: Dañakána, female, age 6

Trial I. 6–30–37. Puts sister doll next to mother doll and father doll far
away. Father doll is next to imaginary fire.

Trial II. 6–31–37. After putting genitals on dolls she moves the dolls around a
little and goes away. Comes back eating. Lays dolls down with their heads on a
toy horn as a pillow and then puts them on toy military tank.

Trial III. 10–13–37. Puts self doll next to grandmother doll. Puts sister doll
next to grandmother doll. Puts father doll on the other side far away and starts
again. Puts sister doll next to father doll, then mother doll, then self doll next to
grandmother doll. Changes positions again. Order now is: self, grandmother,
father, sister, mother. Picks up father doll, moves joints, decapitates.

Trial IV. 10–15–37. Given dolls with sister doll nursing. Takes up father doll
and looks at it. JH: "Does Dañakána nurse?" Simíti: "No." Examiner: "Did
she stop?" Simíti: "Yes." Examiner: "Why?" Simíti: "Because she is grown up."

Examiner: "Maybe she nurses at night." Simíti: "Yes." She puts arms of father doll around self doll and puts sister doll in nursing position.

Trial V. Same day. Not interested.

Trial VI. 10–29–37. Puts well-shaped penis of normal size on father doll. Puts well-shaped breasts on mother doll and on self doll. Does not make vulva for mother doll, self doll, or sister doll. Does not make breasts for sister doll. Throws pellets at Lawésakachiyi, who is looking in. Makes vulvas, all of equal size, for mother, sister, and self.

Trial VII. 11–2–37. Puts breasts and vulva on self doll and vulva on sister doll. Picks up scissors and cuts off part of her own skirt along the edge. Repairs genitals of mother doll. Makes penis on father doll. Tells examiner that Tapáñi and Kayolí had their little boy sleeping partners last night, but that she stayed home because her mother told her to. Says: "Suña, givè me a haircut." Puts sister doll on father doll in nursing position, the father doll lying down. Picks up mother doll and puts it down again. Lays sister doll beside mother doll. Plays with father doll's foot. Says: "I won't take a lover now because I'm fed-up—I'm bored. The boys are violent." Examiner: "Are they all that way?" Simíti: "Yes." Examiner: "Are there any good boys?" Simíti: "There certainly are. I'm not going to take a lover until I'm no longer fed-up with the boys." Her cheeks, however, are painted with two bright red spots. She scratches designs on her legs with the point of the scissors. Scratches designs on the box. Says: "I'll stop now" and goes out. Most of the time was spent chasing swarms of children away from the house.

Trial VIII. 11–5–37. Picks up father doll and then self doll. Puts down self doll. Tries to make father doll stand but it falls every time. Lays it down. Puts fairly well-shaped penis on father doll. Puts vagina on mother doll, sister doll, and self doll. Picks up father doll and improves its penis. A number of children come to the side of the house and look in. Simíti stops playing and sits drawing pictures on the ground. When JH announces that our dinner is cooked Simíti says to the girls: "Go and get your cans—there's rice-water." The girls leave instantly and Simíti picks up father doll and fashions its penis again. Decapitates father doll. Tries to replace head but cannot. Examiner: "Do you want to put the head on again?" Simíti: "Yes." Examiner replaces the head. Simíti stands up father doll and pats its hair, making a smoothing movement with one finger. She keeps pulling the penis—the same smoothing outward gesture with one finger. Lays father doll on mother doll. When the children again look in at the side of the house, Simíti stops dead. She stops playing altogether, whispering "I'll stop."

Pattern of Hostility
  Direction
    1. father
    3. father
    8. father

Forms
　Father: 1) puts far away; 2) decapitates.
Restitution
　of father: tries to insert parts.
Pattern of Sexual Objects
　Direction
　　8. father-self, father-mother
　Forms
　　Father-self: 1) strokes penis.
　　Father-mother: 1) places father on mother.
Other Patterns
　Feature: repressed hostile and sexual strivings toward the father.

DAÑAKÁNA
Age: 6
Sex: female
Sibling: Simíti, female, age 10

Trial I. 10–2–37. Examiner gives Dañakána a self doll that still has a clay penis. In answer to examiner's statement, "This is you," Dañakána says: "No, it has a penis." Dañakána has turtle bite sister doll twice (1). Then she sends out sister doll (2) and says "She is going to urinate." Turtle bites self doll (3).

Trial II. 10–6–37. Dolls are unnamed. After Sorói has manipulated the material Dañakána puts baby doll (no genitals) on father doll *1* close to penis, and says "They're copulating." Examiner: "Is that its father?" Dañakána: "Yes." Dañakána asks whether she can change the father doll to a woman. Examiner says "Do whatever you want to." Dañakána changes the penis to a vulva pressing down the clay and then using a straw. She sets the baby doll on its shoulder.

Trial III. 10–13–37. Looks at Simíti. Simíti is standing near, a poisonous expression on her face, her lips set. Simíti wants to play. Dañakána puts self doll next to mother doll, sister doll next to self, and father doll next to mother doll. Picks up turtle and says: "Look at Simíti's water pot." Simíti has a can in her hand. Dañakána has turtle bite sister doll (1). Every time the sister doll falls Dañakána picks it up and again the turtle bites the sister doll (2). She picks up sister doll and says "My sister's cute little breasts." Puts down sister doll. Picks up father doll and makes it walk. Says: "The cute little thing." Continues to play with father doll. Encircles its head with its arms and tries again to make it walk. Kayolí takes the father doll from Dañakána. Dañakána makes the mother doll walk. Gives mother doll to Kayolí. Calls it Simíti (3), and says "Oh, I made a mistake." Now she adds the sister doll to the group on the ground, and says "Only I remain here" (4). Four girls are boxing. Dañakána sets dolls up in walking position in the following order: sister doll, father doll, mother doll (5). She has encircled self doll on the box with her arms. Puts self doll on father doll's shoulder.

Takes self doll off father doll and tries to place self doll on mother doll. When it does not stay she puts self doll back on shoulders of father doll. Asks for a different doll and it becomes the self doll. It already has a penis, so she presses it down to make it into a vulva. Puts self doll on ground beside sister doll. Order of dolls on ground in marching order is: sister, self, father, mother. JH now gives Dañakána grandmother doll. Dañakána forms clay blob between legs of grandmother doll into a vulva by putting a groove in it. Puts a burden on father doll's arms and again improves vulva of grandmother doll by putting a groove in it with her finger nail. Kayolí has taken the father doll. Dañakána asks for it and Kayolí gives it to her. Dañakana puts all the dolls into the box, saying "Their house." Stands self doll next to mother doll. Grandmother doll is in corner by itself, some distance away from the family group. Order of family group: mother, self, father, sister. Lays mother doll down, saying "She lies down to no purpose." She complains that the penis of the father doll is no good and gives the doll to JH to improve the penis. JH gives it back, saying: "You do it." Now the women who have been out getting forest fruits come back, and all the children except Dañakána and Tanorow'í leave. Dañakána improves penis of father doll. Puts self doll next to grandmother doll, then puts sister doll next to self doll, then mother and then father. Takes dolls out of box and puts them on top. Tanorow'í leaves and Dañakána remains alone. Lifts up father doll and arranges penis. Says "I'll stop."

Trial IV. 10–15–37. Turtle bites self (1), then sister (2), and Dañakána says "Look, it bit Simíti." After another movement of the turtle she says "Simíti" (3). Directs turtle to father (4), then twice to mother (5), and then self (6); says "Ha! Simíti." Turtle bites mother (7), self (8), father (9), mother (10), self (11), sister (12). Sister doll falls down. Turtle bites self (13), and knocks down sister twice (14). Turtle knocks down self (15) and mother (16). Turtle bites father (17), knocks down self (18), bites sister (19) and mother (20), then father (21).

Trial V. 10–29–37. Simíti stops and Dañakána plays. Simíti puts self doll on lap of mother doll and places Dañakána doll near father doll, sitting between its legs, on the ground. Dañakána removes Simíti doll from lap of mother doll and puts it on the ground away from the play table. Asks for turtle "so it can bite." Examiner gives it to her. Dañakána puts sister doll standing up near mother doll. Simíti tells her to stop playing because they want to play with the toy parachute. Dañakána stops.

Trial VI. 10–31–37. Dañakána says she does not know how to make the penis for the father doll. Examiner makes penis for the father doll. Dañakána makes breasts for mother doll. It already has breasts but Dañakána makes better ones. When one is finished she says "Look, it is cute and beautiful." Examiner admires it and Dañakána makes the other one. Both are beautifully made. Dañakána now makes breasts for sister doll. They are small but very well formed. Says: "Soon Simíti will menstruate for the first time." She is about to put breasts on self doll, but stops short and plays with piece of clay. She makes four forms in a kind of square 🔲 with breastlike forms on the corners. She then makes of the clay a narrow strip about four inches long and an eighth of an inch wide and says it is a belt. She has put self doll inside the box. Now she puts the belt around self doll and still keeps it hidden in the box. Yátakana looks in and Dañakána points her out to examiner. Examiner: "Shall I let her in?" Dañakána: "Yes." Examiner: "Shall I keep her out?" Dañakána: "Yes." Examiner: "Are you going to put breasts on yourself?" Dañakána smiles and lies down on the ground embarrassed. She starts to make breasts for self doll and then says "I won't do it. I'll stop." She goes home.

Trial VII. 11–5–37. Picks up sister doll. Dañakána turns away from examiner and lies down prone. Puts vulva on sister doll. Removes it and says "I don't know how." When examiner offers to make it, Dañakána says "Yes." Gives examiner sister doll. Examiner makes vulva for sister doll and self doll, then asks "Shall I make one for the mother too?" Dañakána: "Yes." Examiner: "Large or small?" Dañakána: "Large." Examiner asks Dañakána whether she knows how to make breasts, and Dañakána says "Yes." She takes the sister doll but makes no breasts. Simíti comes to door and looks in. Dañakána puts sister doll back on box and takes self doll, but does not make breasts. She leaves the clay on the box. While Simíti is at the door Dañakána lies on the ground tense, doing nothing. She seems completely squelched. JH calls Simíti to him away from the door, tempting her with a bubble pipe. Dañakána immediately picks up sister doll and puts it with self doll, saying "They go down to the water to bathe." She seems much relieved now that her sister has gone. She walks the dolls off together side by side. Heaps up the earth so that the dolls will stand. Picks up self doll and says "Give it a shirt." Picks up sister doll and says "They have come back." Puts both dolls on the box, side by side. On the other side of self doll is the father doll; on the other side of the sister doll is the mother doll. Dañakána goes out, saying "I'm going to move my bowels, but I'll come back again." When she returns she asks for the widow doll. Examiner tells her that the widow cannot come out yet. Dañakána picks up the scissors but puts them down again. She lies on the ground with her face on the box and sings a dance song. She picks up self doll and fingers the place where the breasts should be. Puts doll back on box. Lies in the same position as before, singing, the edge of the box in her mouth. Keeps looking at the dolls all the time. Turns over on her back and sings, ignoring the dolls. Asks examiner to draw a picture of her. Examiner does so and then Dañakána goes back to the dolls. She picks up the father doll, removes its arms, and says "Crippled." She laughs. Replaces the members and says "Look, I know how." Puts father doll on the ground and makes it stand. Turns it upside down, putting it in the leapfrog position, and makes it turn a somersault. Puts sister doll on ground and says "She's diving." Turns back on sister doll and takes self doll. When JH comes in at the door Dañakána swiftly seizes the sister doll and puts it back into her hand with the self doll. JH goes out and Dañakána puts sister doll back. Then she puts self doll near sister doll and says "I know how to dive."

Pattern of Hostility

Direction

1. sister (3 times), self
2. father
3. sister (repeatedly), sister, mother, all
4. self, sister (twice), father, mother (twice), sister, mother, self, father, mother, self, sister, self, sister (twice), self, mother, father, self, sister, mother, father
5. sister

Forms

Sister: 1) turtle bites; 2) sends out; 3) gives it away; 4) (verbal) "Look, it bit Simíti"; 5) (verbal) "Ha! Simíti"; 6) removes from lap of mother doll; 7) puts on ground away from play table.

Mother: 1) turtle bites; 2) gives it away; 3) (verbal) "I thought it was Simíti."

Father: 1) turtle bites; 2) removes arms; 3) (verbal) "Crippled"; 4) changes penis to vulva.

Self: 1) turtle bites.

All: 1) puts on ground; 2) (verbal) "Only I am here"; 3) puts in marching order.

Restitution

of sister: "My sister's cute little breasts"; puts back in hand; replaces on play box.

Pattern of Sexual Objects

Direction: Self-Father

Forms

Father-self: 1) puts baby doll on father doll; 2) (verbal) "They're copulating."

KAYOLÍ

> Age: 8
> Sex: female
> Siblings: Lorosétina, female, age 20
> Kapíetn, male, age 3½

Trial I. 6–26–37. Says mother doll is pregnant. Slings toy horn on father doll's shoulder. Puts self doll on one shoulder of father doll and brother doll on the other. Arranges dolls in sleeping position: father, mother, brother, self. Mother and father dolls face each other. Lays father doll on side facing mother doll and sees to it that father doll's penis touches mother doll's genital *1*. She has put self doll behind father doll facing its back, and brother doll on other side of mother doll.

Trial II. 6–27–37. Says that mother doll hit father doll because he made a new wife.

Trial III. 10–11–37. After a minute or so she reaches for self doll but takes her hand away. After another little while she asks for mother doll's blouse. When given it she puts it on the mother doll and asks the examiner to help. Arranges father doll's hand. At examiner's suggestion she hesitantly puts brother doll to nurse at breast of mother doll. Her brother comes into the house weeping. She knocks him down. Another little girl seizes him and claps both her hands over his mouth to silence him.

Trial IV. 10–13–37. JH gives her the mother doll. She says of father doll "No penis." JH gives her clay. She makes penis for father doll. It is very flat with a slight projection that looks like a breast. Makes a vulva on self doll. It is just a blob. Puts breasts on mother doll. Says: "I'll make my breasts." Puts breasts on self doll. Mother doll's vulva is a blob. It is very much like the penis of the father doll. Puts brother doll next to mother doll. Asks for turtle. Naichó shows examiner her food every once in awhile. The turtle makes 30 moves, none of which appear to be directed. With the exception of one move against the father all the moves are either away from the dolls or against the self. Then an old man comes to be treated and Kayolí says "Give him something to eat or he'll sorcerize you later." She now makes 26 movements with the turtle; 17 away from the dolls, 4 against the self doll, 3 against the brother, and 2 against the mother. She points out brother doll which she has knocked over on its head. She puts brother doll in nursing position with self doll next to mother doll. She now makes 135 movements with the turtle, as follows: away, 88; self, 22; brother, 4; mother 21. Then the turtle strikes the mother doll twice while she really tries to get at the brother doll. Then the turtle moves as follows: away, 6; mother, 2; father 7. She tries definitely to have the turtle bite the brother doll. Then the turtle moves as follows: away, 10; mother, 3; father, 7; brother, 1; self, 5. She picks up brother doll and looks at it. Remarks on hair on head of brother doll. Examines turtle closely. Then the turtle moves as follows: away, 6; mother, 6; father, 15; brother, 7; self, 1. She makes a definite attempt to have the turtle bite the brother doll. Stops and says "I'll stop."

Summary of movements with turtle: away, 52%; mother, 13%; father, 11%; brother, 6%; self, 17%.

Trial V. Same day. Picks up father doll and plays with the hand. Leaves the vulva on the baby doll. Changes the vagina of the mother doll to a penis.

Trial VI. 11–4–37. Puts vagina on mother doll and penis on father doll. Says: "Intercourse" 1, and puts father doll on mother doll, which is lying face up. Carefully puts penis into vulva and says "Look, intercourse." Asks for "Lorosétina's husband." Examiner gives her another doll. Kayolí puts a penis on it and puts the doll down. Makes a breast of clay and puts it on her own real body, over her breast, which has not yet started to swell. Says: "Don't put your arm around the little girls from other villages—only our village." Raises her own blouse and makes another breast. Removes hands from father doll (1) and says "No hands." Replaces them. Removes a hand (2) and replaces it. Says she wants to decapitate the father doll. Examiner tells her how and she does (3). Kayolí wants to replace head but says she does not know how. Examiner offers to do it and Kayolí tells examiner to hurry. Kayolí puts father doll next to mother doll. Picks up scissors and makes cutting movements across her own forehead (4). Cuts part of her own blouse. Cuts her finger nail. In doing so she snips her finger and says "Ouch!" Cuts her nail again. Puts scissors down and picks up brother-in-law doll, i.e., sister's husband doll. Stands it up with sister doll standing beside it. Holds sister doll in hand. Picks up scissors. Puts down sister, picks up brother-in-law doll and pretends to cut its hair with the scissors (5). Puts doll down and says "I'll cut your penis" (6). Puts down scissors. Makes breasts for her own body. Puts them on over her own real breasts and says: "The same as Simíti's cute little breasts." Simíti is looking in at the door making mouth noises. Simíti wants to play with the dolls. Kayolí places the dolls in the following order: sister's husband, sister, brother, self, father, mother, all lying on their backs next to one another in a row. She draws a design for a poncho on the ground. Then she draws a donkey. Picks up scissors and moves it up and down between mother doll's legs touching the vulva (7). Picks up brother doll and says "I'll cut off its leg" and wants to cut off the leg (8). Repeats "I'll really cut it off." Examiner tells her to go ahead if she wants to. Kayolí again warns examiner that she will really cut it off. She is holding the brother doll up by one leg all the time. Examiner asks Kayolí whether it is really her brother's leg she is going to cut off, and she replies: "The figure of a white woman." She puts everything down and goes out.

Pattern of Hostility

   Direction

    2. father, mother

    5. In this experiment the following symbols have been used for the dolls in order to make the pattern easier to follow: m, mother; a, away; f, father; b, brother; s, self. The brackets have been inserted in order to show where there is a shift in patterning of the movement. [s a s a (twice) f a s a (3 times) s (3 times) a (4 times) s a (5 times) s (twice) a (4 times) s a (7 times) s (twice) a (4 times) s a (twice)] [b m b m b a (twice) ma b a (4 times) b] [a (3 times) s a (4 times) m a (5 times) s (twice) a (twice) s (twice) m a s (twice) a (8 times) m b s a (6 times) s a (4 times) m s a (4 times) s m (3 times) a (4 times) s (5 times) a s a (3 times) s a m (3 times) s a (twice) m (twice) a (3 times) m (twice) b m (3 times) s m a (6 times) m (twice) s a (9 times) s a (10 times) m a (5 times) b a (5 times) m s m (twice) a] [f a f (twice) a f a f (3 times)] [m (twice) a (twice) f b s m b m (twice) a] [f a f (3 times) a (3 times) f a (5 times) f s f s (3 times)] [a b f (twice) m f (4 times) a (twice) f (3 times) a f (3 times) s a (twice) b a f m (3 times) b m b (twice)].

Examination of the patterns of movement of the turtle in this trial shows that they are not random. At first they were concentrated on the self (first set of brackets); then on the mother and brother (second set of brackets); then on the mother and self (third set); then on the father (fourth set); random movements (fifth set); father (sixth set); family (seventh set). A striking feature is the absence of any movement toward the Lorosétina doll.

6. father (3 times), self, brother-in-law, mother, brother

Forms

Brother: 1) turtle bites; 2) makes very definite movements with turtle; 3) repeatedly threatens to cut off leg.

Mother: 1) (verbal) says that mother hit father because he made a new wife; 2) turtle bites; 3) removes hands; 4) (verbal) "no hands"; 5) expresses wish to decapitate; 6) changes vulva to penis; 7) makes cutting movements on vulva.

Father: 1) (verbal) says that mother hit father because he made a new wife; 2) turtle bites; 3) amputates; 4) decapitates.

Sister:

Brother-in-law: 1) pretends to cut hair; 2) (verbal) "I'll cut your penis."

Restitution

of brother: puts to nurse.
of father: inserts parts.

Pattern of Sexual Objects

Direction

3. father-mother
6. father-mother

Forms

Father-mother: 1) puts genitalia in contact; 2) (verbal) "Look, intercourse."

Other Patterns

Feature: preoccupation with breasts.

KAPÍETN

Age: 3 years, 6 months
Sex: Male
Siblings: Lorosétina, female, age 20
Kayolí, female, age 8

Trial I. 11–5–37. Puts mother doll near father doll and says "Stays near spouse." The Lorosétina doll is lying beside and touching the back of the mother doll. Kapíetn says "They're copulating" *1*. Sits awhile and at last says "I'll stop." He leaves.

Pattern of Hostility
    None

Pattern of Sexual Objects
    Direction
        1. sister-mother

    Forms
        Sister-mother: 1) (verbal) "they're copulating."

SORÓI

        Age: 7
        Sex: female
        Sibling: Tórot, male, age 10

Trial I. 6–26–37. Puts mother doll next to father doll. Puts brother doll on other side of mother doll and puts self doll on other side of father doll. Puts toy horn under father doll's head. Puts penis on father doll, and says "Now they will have intercourse" *1*. Examines mother doll and says "No genital." Examiner gives her clay with which to make vulva. Sorói lays father doll on mother doll *2*, and exclaims: "Look, it just fits!" The vulva and the penis meet.

Trial II. 6–29–37. She does not like the badly made vulva of the mother doll. Examiner gives Sorói more clay and she makes a better vulva. Puts father doll on mother doll *1*, taking care to put the father doll's penis into the mother doll's vagina. Puts two toy horns on father doll's shoulder calling them guns. Puts breasts on mother doll. She shapes them very well and makes them seem part of the body by smoothing them down until they are flush with the body—as though there were no change in texture between the body of the doll and the breasts. Puts the dolls in sleeping position: father, mother, self, brother. Imaginary camp fire is next to father doll. She has put tremendous nipples on mother doll's breasts. She now models a little tiger of clay, making tiny punctures in the body to represent spots. Then she says the mother doll is going to have a baby. Examiner: "Perhaps later." Sorói: "Tonight."

Trial III. 10–6–37. Dolls are unnamed. Sorói takes breasts off mother doll (1) and puts them on a smaller doll. She tries to put breasts on a baby doll but gives up, saying "The cute little thing." Puts breasts on a larger doll. Removes the vulva from mother doll and uses the clay to make breasts for the mother doll. [Dañakána now manipulates the material. Her last move is to put a baby doll on the shoulder of the father doll.] Sorói puts the turtle on top of all the dolls Dañakána is playing with. Darotoyí comes along and Sorói directs the turtle to him. When he tries to touch it Sorói becomes angry and says to the turtle "Kill him! Kill him!" She asks the examiner to decapitate the father doll and put the head where the hand should be. Sorói does it (2), removing both hands, and says "Look, it died" (3). She puts it together again. Arranges the family: mother, four child dolls, father. This is all the dolls there are.

Trial IV. 10–11–37. Squashes penis of father doll (1). Stretches óut the arms and tries to make it stand. Puts father doll next to mother doll. Lays mother doll on arm of father doll. Starts to put self doll in arms of mother doll but lays self doll down. Turtle bites as follows: mother (2), father (3), self (4), mother (5), father (6). Turtle moves away (7) and then moves as follows: mother (twice) (8), away (9), brother (8), father (9), mother (twice) (10).

Trial V. 10–13–37. She makes a blob for the penis of brother doll. It looks like a breast. Puts definite vagina on self doll. Picks up turtle and it makes 44 moves: 13 against the father, 8 against the mother, 4 against the brother, 4 against the self, and 15 are away from the dolls. The one clearly directed move is against the self.

Trial VI. 11–4–37. Uses scissors to cut clay. Makes a breast which she changes to a penis, changes back to a breast, puts down on the box, pressing it out of shape. Stands father doll up and plays with the joints. Stops and goes home. Other little girls were looking in all around the house.

Pattern of Hostility
  Direction
    3. mother (twice), father (twice)
    4. father, mother, father, self, mother, father, mother (twice), brother, father, mother (twice)
    5. father (3 times), mother, brother, self, father (3 times), mother, self, mother, brother (twice), father, self, brother, brother, father (twice), father (3 times) mother, father, self, mother (3 times), self, mother

Forms
  Mother: 1) turtle bites; 2) removes breasts.
  Brother: 1) turtle bites.
  Father: 1) asks examiner to decapitate father doll and put the head in place of the hand; 2) decapitates father doll and puts head in place of hand; 3) removes both hands; 4) (verbal) "It died"; 5) squashes penis; 6) turtle bites.
  Self: 1) turtle bites.

  Restitution
    of mother: restores breasts.
    of father: parts inserted.

Pattern of Sexual Objects
  Direction
    1. father-mother (twice)
    2. father-mother
  Forms
    Father-mother: 1) (verbal) "Now they will have intercourse"; 2) lays father doll on mother doll; 3) (verbal) "It just fits."

CHAUPÁ

Age: 12–13
Sex: female
Siblings: Kanaidí, male, age 9½
Darotoyí, male, age 4
Simkoolí, female, age 1

Trial I. 6–27–37. Looks for genital of mother doll. Abandons dolls.
Trial II. 10–15–37. Indiscriminate waving of turtle. Says: "Look!" Turtle moves as follows: self, Kanaidí. She looks up. Turtle moves as follows: mother twice, baby twice, mother, baby, self, mother, baby twice, self. Seven-eighths of her movements with the turtle are away from the dolls.

KANAIDÍ

Age: 9½
Sex: male
Siblings: Chaupá, female, age 12–13
Darotoyí, male, age 4
Simkoolí, female, age 1

Trial I. 10–2–37. Is admitted to house after clamoring to come in. Picks up dolls. Starts to move turtle about. Has turtle bite father doll twice, then says "Well, I'm finished now," and goes out of the house saying, "Well, I'm happy now."

DAROTOYÍ

Age: 4
Sex: male
Siblings: Chaupá, female, age 12–13
Kanaidí, male, age 9½
Simkoolí, female, age 1

Trial I. 10–2–37. Kanaidí has turtle bite father doll twice. Then he says "Well, I'm finished now," and goes out of the house, saying: "Well, I'm happy now." Darotoyí has turtle bite baby doll's genital over and over again, and says "Vulva, vulva, vulva, vulva, bitten" (1). He has turtle make a very vicious attack on head of mother doll (2). The turtle bites with a bang as Darotoyí pushes it violently against mother doll's head. Turtle again bites baby doll (3). [Lapse of a few minutes while Yorodaikolík manipulates the material and both he and Darotoyi waver between going away and remaining.] Darotoyí has turtle bite mother doll's head (4) and father doll's penis (5). He puts turtle on father doll directly on the penis. Now, still keeping the turtle on the father doll, he pushes it up to the father doll's eyes (6) and says "Look, it bit his eyes. It's already swallowed them." Has turtle bite brother doll's penis (7). Says: "Look it swallowed Kanaidí's penis." [Darotoyí and Yorodaikolík again waver between going home and remaining.] Darotoyí puts father doll on mother doll, saying "They're having intercourse" *1*. Yorodaikolík says "Simkoolí is yelling because her mother is having intercourse."

Trial II. Puts self doll on mother doll *1*, penis in vagina. Puts self doll on sister doll in same position *2*. Has mother doll walk away. Has self doll follow mother doll by pushing self doll along after mother doll. Has father doll perform intercourse with brother doll *3*, and then with sister doll *4*. Lifts up father doll and says "This is toad's food." Puts brother doll on father doll's lap and says: "Go!" Examiner: "Where are they going?" Darotoyí: "To the sugar cane plantation."

Trial III. 10–13–37. Moves joints of father doll. Makes arm encircle figure and meet hand in front. Tries to make it stand but it will not. Changes position of arms. Lays it down on back. Lays mother doll on outstretched arm of father doll. Sets up sister doll and puts it on another chair. Brings it back and lays it next to mother doll. Takes it away. Puts down mother doll. Moves joints of father doll. Sets it up on all fours. He stops. Naichó has been looking daggers at him all the time.

Trial IV. 10–14–37. Picks up father doll. Says that brother doll has no penis. Examiner makes one. Darotoyí puts father doll on all fours and tells examiner to look. Darotoyí picks up father doll and plays with joints. Touches penis of father doll and puts down father doll. Picks up mother doll and makes it walk away. JH: "Why does it go away?" Darotoyí: "My father follows her." Picks up father doll and puts it in back of mother doll. Puts father doll on top of mother doll *1*. Mátakana says "Spouses now." Darotoyí very carefully puts penis of father doll in contact with vagina of mother doll *2*. He lays them down carelessly to one side and puts baby doll to nurse. Turns father doll upside down on all fours. He treats it like a shelter, putting all the dolls under the father doll. Says: "It is raining." Picks up father again and plays with it.

Trial V. 10–15–37. Turtle bites mother doll (1). Examiner tells Darotoyí to put baby doll at mother's breast. He does. Darotoyí directs turtle to bite brother doll (2). Directs turtle to bite self doll (3). Again directs turtle to bite brother doll (4). Directs turtle to bite sister doll (5). Turtle bites self doll (6) and Darotoyi laughs. Turtle bites self doll 4 times (7), then brother doll (8), and then sister doll (9). Darotoyí looks at brother doll. Sets sister doll up on its feet and turtle bites it (10). Has turtle bite baby doll (11) by putting turtle on mother doll. Turtle bites sister doll (12), self (13), baby 4 times (14), mother (15). Darotoyí says "vulva." Turtle bites sister doll (16) and then baby doll (17). Examiner puts baby doll to nurse. Turtle bites brother doll (18), then father doll (19). Darotoyí says "He died. Die." Examiner: "Did he die?" Darotoyí: "Yes. Kanaidí's penis is bitten" (20). Examiner: "Do you want to nurse?" Darotoyí: "Simkoolí's companion." Puts self doll to breast of mother doll. Turtle bites vulva of sister doll (21), then brother doll (22). He has turtle bite self doll (23) in the anus by lifting up the turtle. Self doll falls off play table and Darotoyí puts it back, saying "You also nurse." Turtle bites mother doll in anus (24) and then bites self doll (25). Turtle bites brother doll (26) and Darotoyí says "It bit Kanaidí! It bit Kanaidí! It bit Kanaidí! It bit Kanaidí! My father is bitten (27). *Kum!* Her vulva." Turtle bites sister doll (28). Darotoyí: "Her vulva. Look! Chaupá. My mother (29). It bit Simkoolí's thigh (30). It bit my father (31). It bit Chaupá (32). It bit Kanaidí" (33).

Pattern of Hostility

 Direction

   1. baby, mother, baby, mother, father, brother
   2. father, brother, father
   5. mother, brother, self, brother, sister, self, self (4 times), brother, sister, sister, baby, sister, self, baby (4 times), mother, sister, baby, brother, father, brother, sister, brother, self, mother, self, brother, father, sister, mother, baby, father, sister, brother

 Forms

   Baby: 1) turtle bites; 2) (verbal) "Vulva, vulva, vulva, vulva, bitten"; 3) (verbal) "It bit Simkoolí's thigh."

   Mother: 1) turtle bites; 2) (verbal) "My mother."

   Father: 1) turtle bites; 2) (verbal) "Look, it bit his eyes"; 3) (verbal) "This is toad's food"; 4) (verbal) "Go"; 5) (verbal) "He died"; 6) (verbal) "My father is bitten."

   Sister: 1) turtle; 2) (verbal) "Her vulva."

   Brother: 1) turtle bites; 2) (verbal) "Look, it swallowed Kanaidí's penis"; 3) puts on father's lap; 4) (verbal) "Go"; 5) (verbal) "Kanaidí's penis is bitten; 6) (verbal) "It bit Kanaidí. It bit Kanaidí. It bit Kanaidí. It bit Kanaidí."

   Self: 1) turtle bites.

Pattern of Sexual Objects

 Direction

   1. father-mother
   2. self-mother; self-sister; father-brother; father-sister
   4. father-mother

 Forms

   Father-mother: 1) father on mother; 2) (verbal) "They are having intercourse."

   Mother-self: 1) self on mother

   Sister-self: 1) self on sister

   Father-brother: 1) father on brother

   Father-sister: 1) father on sister

KUWASIÑÍTN

Age: 8
Sex: male
Siblings: Walíetn, male, age 14
Katinorodí, male, age 10½

Trial I. 10–15–37. The following material is extracted from an experiment in which the dolls were set up to represent Nakínak's family. There are the following dolls: mother, father, baby sister, [elder] brother, Nakínak. Kuwasiñítn, Nakínak, Yorodaikolík, and Wetél manipulate the material.

Wetél puts brother doll on Nakínak doll and then on father doll. Kuwasiñítn says "Tiny anus." Puts brother doll on father doll *1*, penises touching. Puts penis of brother doll in his own mouth *2*. Puts father doll on mother doll in position of intercourse *3*. Puts Nakínak doll on father doll *4*. Puts huge vulva on baby doll. Puts breasts on father doll. Puts father doll on mother doll, saying "Oma'í[15] is having intercourse" *5*. Puts father doll on mother doll *6* and brother doll on top of father doll *7*. Puts father doll next to brother doll, then changes it and lays the Nakínak doll next to father doll. Picks up father doll and lays it on mother doll *8*, saying "Intercourse." Says: "He is praying."[16] The penis falls off the Nakínak doll and Kuwasiñítn puts one on. When Kuwasiñítn says that Nakínak's mother and father are having intercourse Nakínak does not respond. "Adíechi's[17] mother," says Kuwasiñítn putting the brother doll and the mother doll in copulating position *9*. He removes the brother doll. He puts the brother doll on top of the mother and father dolls *10* and Nakínak shakes the box. Kuwasiñítn takes the Nakínak doll from Nakínak and begins to make a penis for it.

Pattern of Hostility

   Direction

     1. Uncertain

   Forms

     Uncertain: 1) (verbal) "Tiny anus."

Pattern of Sexual Objects

   Direction

     1. Brother-father, brother-self, father-mother, father-self, father-mother (twice), brother-father (piling), father-mother, brother-mother, brother (father-mother) (piling)

   Forms

     Brother-father: 1) puts brother on father, penises touching; 2) (piling) puts brother on father.

     Brother-self: 1) puts penis of brother doll in own real mouth.

[15] Nakínak's father.
[16] Or simply "He has his head in his hands." This is the more likely translation.
[17] Adíechi is Nakínak's step-sibling.

Father-self: 1) puts Nakínak doll on father doll.

Father-mother: 1) puts in position of intercourse; 2) (verbal) "Oma'i is having intercourse"; 3) (verbal) "Intercourse."

Brother-mother: 1) puts in position of intercourse.

MARALÚ
Age: 12
Sex: male
Sibling: Wetél, male, age 6

Trial I. 10–6–37. Girls are playing with the dolls. Examiner says to Maralú: "Would you like to play with the dolls?"

"I don't like to."

"Isn't it the custom for boys to play with dolls?"

"It's a girl's custom."

Maralú moves closer to the group of girls. He joins the group. Puts father doll on top of mother doll and says "They're having intercourse." Rides the toy tank over them. Picks up father doll and removes a hand. Replaces it. Removes the head. Replaces it. Holds the father doll by the feet and swings it head down just as they do with young birds that they catch and torment. Says: "I'll stop now." Repairs penis of father doll, saying "No testicles." Again puts mother and father dolls in position of intercourse, the legs of the father doll between the legs of the mother doll. He pushes the father doll back and forth. Goes away. He wants to play with the bubble pipe.

WETÉL
Age: 6
Sex: male
Sibling: Maralú, male, age 12

Trial I. 10–11–37. Turtle bites father, mother, brother (3 times), self, mother, brother (twice), mother, brother. Almost knocks brother doll off the board. Puts brother doll next to mother doll. Removes and puts self next to mother doll. Turtle bites mother, self, brother, mother twice. Examiner: "Why was the mother bitten?" Wetél: "Because it doesn't like her."

Trial II. 10–15–37. Asks for father doll first. JH says there are no genitals on any of the dolls, and gives Wetél clay. Wetél puts very small, round, breast-like penis on father doll. Puts good penis on self doll and takes a longer time to do it. Puts good penis on brother doll. Says: "Now, Jolio, the woman." Kuwasiñítn says "A great big vulva." Wetél puts a very large and badly made vulva and large breasts on the mother doll. He sticks his own head and shoulders into the play box. Points to brother doll and says: "Nakínak has a big belly, *piyátin*[18] his penis." Nakínak says of one of the dolls, "It has no hair." Wetél calls him "Dog."

[18] Meaning uncertain.

Trial III. Same day. The following material is extracted from an experiment in which the dolls were set up to represent Nakínak's family. There are the following dolls: mother, father, baby sister [elder] brother, self. Nakínak, Yorodaikolík, Kuwasiñítn, and Wetél manipulate the material.

JH puts baby doll to nurse. Wetél says "Oma'í's[19] penis." Wetél puts brother doll on top of mother doll. Puts brother doll on Nakínak doll, then on father doll. Very carefully puts penis of Nakínak doll into anus of brother doll. Puts baby doll face down on mother doll in position of intercourse. Puts brother doll on mother doll, saying "He has intercourse." Puts penis of brother doll into anus of Nakínak doll, saying "He has intercourse in the anus." Nakínak takes brother doll off self doll. Wetél growls and says "He is having intercourse," and replaces the dolls. Wetél puts Nakínak doll on mother doll. Tries to spread legs of mother doll but cannot. Puts Nakínak doll on mother doll, penis in vagina. Puts brother doll on top of Nakínak doll, saying "He has intercourse," naming the dolls as he puts them in position. He uses the names of Nakínak and Nakínak's brother. Puts Nakínak doll on baby doll, saying "Nakínak has intercourse with his sister." After a few moments he says "I'll have intercourse with you." Nakínak sets up brother doll, but Wetél snatches it, saying of the baby doll, "Where are its feet? Where is its vulva? Jolio, it has no vulva."

Trial IV. 11–5–37. Makes penis for brother doll and self doll. Asks for forest fruit which is lying near. When examiner gives him some he says "I'll stop," and goes out.

Pattern of Hostility

Direction

1. father, mother, brother (3 times), self, mother, brother (twice), mother, brother (twice), mother, self, brother, mother (twice)
2. brother

Forms

Mother: 1) turtle bites; 2) (verbal) "It doesn't like her."
Father: 1) turtle bites.
Brother: 1) turtle bites; 2) (verbal) "Nakínak has a big belly."
Self: 1) turtle bites.

TANOROW'Í

Age: 10
Sex: female
Sibling: Masénkena, female, age 16

Trial I. 10–9–37. Puts father doll behind mother doll in position of intercourse *1*, and arranges them very carefully so the genitalia meet. She says "They are having intercourse." She puts the self doll on the other side of the mother doll in nursing position and says "I am nursing, more's the pity." Interruption while

---

[19] Name of Nakínak's father.

Yorodaikolík manipulates the material. His last move is to put the doll representing himself on the mother doll with the penis very carefully placed in the
vagina of the mother doll. Tanorow'í puts the mother doll and the father doll in
position of intercourse *2*, the self doll next to them, i.e., the father doll is on top
of the mother doll, but the arm of the father doll is stretched over the self doll.
Tanorowí points to the father doll and says "Look, my father." Pointing to the
self doll she says "It's crying." Examiner: "Why is it crying?" Tanorow'í: "Because they are having intercourse." She leaves dolls in position of intercourse and
turns to blowing bubbles. Yatákana removes the father doll, whereupon Tanorow'í
who seemed completely engrossed in bubble blowing yells "Leave it alone!" She
replaces the father doll. While she is blowing bubbles a doll falls on the ground
and she says "The poor little (female) thing." Another girl now asks to play with
the dolls and takes them, but Tanorow'í retains self doll, saying "It stays with
me."

Trial II. 11–1–37. Takes a long time to put genital on sister doll. First she puts
a blob on the doll and then uses a piece of reed which she inserts as though it were
a penis to make an opening in the genital. The mother doll already has a vagina.
Tanorow'í, however, inserts reed in the same manner as in the previous doll. Picks
up father doll and moves the arms. Father doll has no penis. Examiner suggests
making one and Tanorow'í does so. She spreads the father doll's legs far apart and
makes a breast-shaped penis. Then she brings the legs together. She plays with
the penis, making the tip a little more definite. Sits down father doll, its back to
her and its legs outspread. Moves it around from place to place. Says: "Suña, I
have no grandmother."[20] The position of the dolls is: father doll (sitting), mother
doll (lying face up), sister doll, self doll, grandmother doll. Makes a genital for the
grandmother doll. So far she has put breasts on none of the dolls. Sits up mother
doll next to father doll and lays the sister doll across the mother doll's legs. Puts
sister doll in nursing position and puts arms of mother doll out to hold it up. The
dolls do not remain in position. Picks up father doll and puts it, legs outspread,
in front of mother doll *1*. Says: "Intercourse," but she does not release the father
doll. Picks up father doll and makes the penis a little longer (it is now beginning to
look like a penis) and sits it down again beside mother doll. Puts self doll in arms
of father doll, face of self doll very close to penis of father doll *2*. Puts sister doll on
legs of mother doll. Puts clay on perineum of mother doll. Lays mother doll on
its side and puts grandmother doll next to it. Takes grandmother doll away and
puts sister doll beside it facing it. Dolls do not remain in position. She tries again.
Puts sister doll beside mother doll facing it, and puts self doll next to anal region
of mother doll. The face of the self doll is against the anal region. Takes self doll
away. Puts father doll back of mother doll *3*. Father doll faces mother doll's back
in position of intercourse. Tries to make penis of father doll enter the mother doll
from behind. Picks up father doll, repairs the penis, and does the same thing.

[20] Or "My grandmother is not around." She is referring to Sokoolí who, she says, is her mother's
mother.

Takes more clay and makes the penis still longer. Again puts father doll behind mother doll. She says the clay she put on mother doll's perineum is "her anus." Tries over and over again to make father doll's penis enter anus of mother doll 4. It works, but she again picks up father doll, manipulates penis and puts it into mother doll's anus 5. Picks up father doll, carefully arranges body so that it will remain in position when she lays it face down. She again puts hole in vulva and anus of mother doll. Picks up father doll and manipulates penis. Lays mother doll down on its face. Lays it on its back beside the father doll which is also on its back. Self doll is next to mother doll on the other side. Order of dolls: father, mother, self, sister, grandmother, all lying on their backs. Tanorow'í has stopped playing because there are many children who want to play looking in. Tanorow'í just sits and looks at them. The girls tear at the reed walls of the house and yell. They will not go away. They dash around crying that the examiner is a wild pig and that they are "angry now."

Pattern of Hostility

No overt patterns

Pattern of Sexual Objects

Direction

1. father-mother, father-mother, father-self
2. father-mother, father-self, mother-self, father-mother (3 times)

Forms

Father-mother: 1) places in dorso-ventral position; 2) (verbal) "They are having intercourse"; 3) places in ventral-ventral position; 4) places father doll in front of mother doll with its legs outspread; 5) (verbal) "Intercourse"; 6) tries to have penis enter anus of mother.

Father-self: 1) places arm of father doll over self while father is in position of intercourse with mother; 2) places self doll in arms of father doll, face close to the penis.

Mother-self: 1) places self doll with face next to anal region of mother.

Other Patterns

Regression: places self in nursing position; (verbal) "I am nursing, more's the pity."

Feature: extreme preoccupation with sex relations of parents. Evidence of oral and genital strivings toward father. Absence of overt hostility.

ÑAKÉTE

Age: 9
Sex: female
Siblings: Mátakana, female, age 3
Hetolí, male, age 15 months

Trial I. 10–11–37. Hetolí is touching the dolls and Ñakéte tells him to stop. He hits her. She stops him again and he goes away. She puts the baby doll in the arms of the mother doll. Puts self doll next to father doll and puts baby doll to nurse. Places self doll close to mother doll.

MÁTAKANA

Age: 3
Sex: female
Siblings: Ñakéte, female, age 9
Hetolí, male, age 15 months

Trial I. 10–14–37. Darotoyí is present. Mátakana has in her hand a large knife, belonging to her parents, which she has been carrying about with her. She threatens Darotoyí with it. She picks up mother doll and turns it around, looks at it, puts it down. Examiner asks her to put baby doll to nurse. She does not do it for a long time. Then she puts it to nurse. It falls down. Yorodaikolík, who is watching, shoots a marble at baby doll. Mátakana repairs bent penis of baby doll. She picks up mother doll, turns it bottom up, and examines its genitalia (?). Sits mother doll down and puts baby doll to nurse. Strokes mother doll's head. Takes hold of father doll's legs and lets go. Is distracted by a little boy who is yelling, "Suña, look! Jolio, look!" Mátakana takes baby doll from breast of mother doll and puts it between mother doll's legs. The wind blows the baby doll away. Mátakana puts baby doll back between legs of mother doll, the head of the baby doll resting on the legs of the mother doll. She is distracted by Darotoyí who is playing with bubble pipe. Mátakana encircles the group of dolls with both her arms and bends her head over them. Darotoyí exchanges his bubble pipe for the dolls.

Trial II. Follows on Trial I by a few minutes. Picks up mother doll and puts baby doll on mother doll's thighs. It is really on the genital. She says, "The product of her vagina" (1). Piles all dolls except father doll on top of mother doll *1*. Repeats. Piles all the dolls on mother doll's back. Picks up baby doll and sister doll and says "My child" (2). Puts baby doll on mother doll's genital and says "It goes into her vagina" (3). Puts baby doll to nurse and puts sister doll on top of mother doll. She observes that one of the dolls that had been used in the preceding experiment with Yatákana is "hard." She puts baby doll in arms of mother doll—not nursing. Puts sister doll next to mother doll. Darotoyí comes to tell examiner that the children playing with the bubble pipe are stingy. Mátakana says "He's going to cry." Mátakana puts sister doll on top of mother doll *2* and father doll on top of all *3*, saying: "They are lying on it (or her)."[21] Takes father doll off and plays with joints. Puts ball on back of father doll in her mouth. Puts father doll down on its back and puts the penis of the baby doll in contact with the penis of the father doll (4) *4*. Puts legs of baby doll on penis of father doll. Holds self doll and ignores sister doll. Picks up sister doll. Puts it down. Puts

[21] The third person personal prefix in Pilagá is the same for masculine, feminine, and neuter.

baby doll on mother doll's arm. Picks up self doll and examines it. Puts baby doll beside sister doll (5) which is beside mother doll. Boys come over and Mátakana looks around at each one in turn. She says "I'll stop," but remains where she is. Plays with joints of father doll and pushes it around face down on ground (6). Turns it over and then picks it up. Puts her mouth against father doll's face. She drops it and walks away.

Trial III. Same day. After Yorodaikolík stops playing, Mátakana indicates that she wants to play by saying "I." She sits down and puts baby doll to nurse (mouth near breast of mother doll, body over genital of mother doll). She plays with joints of father doll. Arm comes off. Mátakana smiles and hands father doll to examiner. JH repairs it. Mátakana kisses sister doll on mouth. Puts mother doll on top of father doll *1* and says "Has intercourse." Puts baby doll on top of mother doll *2* and says "You have intercourse in the anus" (1) *3*. Says: "You have intercourse with milk" and puts baby doll on top of father doll's penis (2) *4*. Puts mouth of mother doll to her own mouth and says to mother doll, "Lie down, you poor little thing." Puts baby doll on top of father doll (3), baby doll's penis on penis of father doll *5*. Says: "At last her vagina is finished" (4), and puts baby doll next to mother doll. Leaves self doll next to baby doll and has sister doll next to self doll. Father doll is on other side of sister doll.

Trial IV. Same day. Sends baby doll away, saying "(Someone's) younger brother." Sends another doll away, saying ("Someone's) younger brother." She leaves one female doll next to mother doll. When examiner asks who it is, Darotoyí says "(Someone's) younger brother" and Mátakana repeats it. She says, "Look, there is no other." Brings back other dolls.

Pattern of Hostility
  Direction
    1. baby
    2. baby (5 times), father
    3. baby, mother, baby (twice)
    4. baby
  Forms
    Baby: 1) puts between mother's legs; 2) (verbal) "The product of her vagina"; 3) (verbal) "My child"; 4) (verbal) "It goes into her vagina"; 5) puts baby on mother; 6) (verbal) "You have intercourse in the anus"; 7) removes baby; 8) (verbal) "You have intercourse with milk"; 9) (verbal) "At last her vagina is finished"; 10) sends away brother and other brothers.
    Mother: 1) (verbal) "The product of her vagina"; 2) puts baby on mother; 3) (verbal) "You have intercourse in the anus"; 4) (verbal) "At last her vagina is finished."
    Father: 1) pushes it around face down on ground.

Restitution

of baby: put to nurse.

of father: gives to examiner to repair.

Pattern of Sexual Objects

Direction

2. (piling) all-mother; (piling) all-mother; (piling) sister-mother, father-all; baby-father.

3. mother-father; baby-mother; baby-father.

Forms

Mother-father: 1) mother on father; 2) (verbal) "Has intercourse."

Mother-baby: 1) baby on mother; 2) (verbal) "You have intercourse in the anus."

Mother-sister: 1) sister on mother.

Father-baby: 1) penis of baby in contact with penis of father; 2) (verbal) "You have intercourse with milk."

Other: 1) piling on mother; 2) (verbal) "They are lying on her."

Other Patterns

Oral behavior: puts mouth against face of father doll. Kisses sister doll. Puts mouth of mother to own real mouth.

Feature: spread of sexuality.

NAKÍNAK

Age: 6

Sex: male

Siblings: Adíechi (step-sib.), male, age 11

Niwéte, female, age 2½

Trial I. 10–15–37. Although this experiment was set up to represent the members of Nakínak's family, the material was manipulated a great deal by Kuwasiñítn, Yorodaikolík and Wetél. The protocol below is an extract of Nakínak's manipulation of the play material and his reaction to it.

JH puts baby doll to nurse. Nakínak sits and does nothing. Then he puts brother doll on mother doll *1*. When Wetél puts brother doll on mother doll Nakínak takes it off scowling. Wetél puts penis of Nakínak doll into anus of brother doll and Yorodaikolík says "They are having intercourse." Nakínak pinches him. This is followed by a long period during which the other boys manipulate the material and Nakínak does nothing. Nakínak next takes up the play after Kuwasiñítn has put the mother and father dolls in position of intercourse and has started to repair the penis of the Nakínak doll. Nakínak sets up the father doll. Yorodaikolík puts it down on all fours. Nakínak sets it on its feet. Kuwasiñítn takes it away. Nakínak sets up the brother doll but it is snatched by Wetél. Nakínak sets up the father doll. He says of the brother doll, "Adíechi."

Takes the brother doll from Kuwasiñítn and puts it aside. Then he tries to put it on top of the mother and father dolls *2*. Kuwasiñítn takes it away but Nakínak puts it back *3*, saying "Nóroi."[22] When Kuwasiñítn puts the brother doll on top of the mother and father dolls, Nakínak shakes the play box. Nakínak puts the self doll next to the baby doll which is next to the mother doll. He tries hard. He starts to put a penis on the self doll. Kuwasiñítn takes the doll away to make a penis. Nakínak sets up the father doll and fixes the penis.

Pattern of Hostility
None

Pattern of Sexual Objects
Direction
1. brother-mother, brother on mother and father twice
Forms
Brother-mother: 1) puts brother on mother.
Brother (father-mother): 1) puts brother on top of father and mother.

ANETOLÍ

Age: 9
Sex: female
Siblings: Wodyáraik, male, age 20[23]
Yatákana, female, age 5
Yalokodítn, male, age 2

Trial I. 11-1-37. Puts beautiful breasts with nipples on mother doll. Starts to put breasts on the Wodyáraik doll. Examiner says "It's a male. It's your elder brother. Are you putting breasts on it?" Anetolí says "Yes." She laughs, and when examiner shows her the self doll, she puts down the Wodyáraik doll and says she will put breasts on herself. She does so. Siwóna puts penis on father doll and lays the doll down on its back. She puts both of the younger sibling dolls on the father doll in nursing position. Siwóna starts to put breasts on Wodyáraik doll. Both girls cooperate in putting breasts on the brother dolls.[24] The girls remark that the dolls are males. Anetolí removes breasts of Wodyáraik doll, but leaves them on the baby doll. Siwóna puts the Anetolí doll to nurse. Anetolí says to her angrily, "Stop it!" Puts vulva on self doll. Cuts her own real skirt with the scissors. Tries to cut head of father doll with the scissors. Lays down father doll, picks up self doll, picks up father doll. Laughs and puts them down again. Picks up self doll and looks at it. Lays it down. Asks examiner to let the other girls come in. Asks over and over again. Examiner lets them come in. Anetolí stops playing with the dolls and cuts the hair of one of the girls. She gives the dolls to Yatákana.

[22] Nóroi is an old woman who lives next door to these boys.
[23] Married and living in a different village.
[24] Not clear who put breasts on the baby doll.

Trial II. 11–2–37. In passing the side of the house where Yatákana is looking in, Anetolí puts her hand through the hole in the wall and aims a blow at her. Anetolí is given the material minus the Wodyáraik doll. The first thing she does is to put large, very well shaped breasts on the self doll. She laughs and says "Its breasts are huge." When she observes the other little girls going for water she leaves to join them.

Trial III. 11–4–37. Stands up father doll. Says: "I'll make breasts for it." Makes breasts and puts them on Wodyáraik doll. Examiner: "Is that your elder brother?" Anetolí: "Yes." She continues putting breasts on the Wodyáraik doll. Says: "Suña's house will be a poor little thing, so empty!"[25] Puts other breast on Wodyáraik doll. Picks up self doll and says "It's heavy. Its face is painted." Puts breasts on sister doll and gives mother doll to Talkóna. She also gives Talkóna clay to make breasts with, and Talkóna very carefully puts breasts on the mother doll. Anetolí makes beautiful breasts with nipples for the sister doll.. Tries to cut Talkóna's skirt with the scissors, but is pushed away. Tries to cut Talkóna's hair, but Talkóna will not let her. Anetolí then cuts the edge of her own skirt. Puts down scissors and picks up sister doll. Examines it, puts it down, picks up scissors and makes cutting movements on her own foot (1). Puts scissors in her own lap and admires father doll's shoes. Tries to make father doll stand but without success. Lays it down. Picks up Wodyáraik doll and then the mother doll. Turns the mother doll over and says "Its anus" (2). Examines head of mother doll. Puts dolls down, takes scissors and cuts the edge of her skirt. Talkóna puts baby doll in arms of father doll and Anetolí throws it down "by accident" (3). Anetolí puts sister doll there instead. She still holds the scissors and is trying to cut the wooden play box. She wants to place the mother and father dolls in position of intercourse *1* but they have no genitals. She removes a breast from the mother doll and makes a penis for the father doll. She removes the other breast and makes a vulva. Talkóna picks up baby doll and says to it, "Nurse." Anetolí puts penis of father doll into vagina of mother doll *2*. Legs fall off father doll and when Anetolí tries to replace them the penis falls off. She says "It's good that way" (4). Leaves the legs off and replaces the penis. Replaces the legs. Examiner asks the two girls why they have no sleeping partners and Anetolí replies "We are afraid." Talkóna adds, "Men's big penises injure our vaginas and then we menstruate and bleed." Anetolí says that the older brother is pregnant. Examiner says, "But it's a male." Talkóna says, "This one (mother doll) is pregnant." The mother and father dolls are still in position of intercourse. Talkóna continues, "Maralú was my sleeping partner but I became angry. He wanted to have intercourse with me but it was no good and so he went home. He was angry." She puts baby doll on sister doll and says "Intercourse with a relative." Anetolí, very much amused, says "Look, Yatákana and her younger brother are having intercourse, they are copulating" *3*. She again picks up the mother and father dolls and says, "They have intercourse a great deal" *4* (5). Picks up self doll, looks at it awhile, puts it down. Talkóna has been improving the breasts of the Wodyáraik doll (elder brother). Anetolí takes the doll from her and continues improving the breasts. Examiner: "I thought it was your elder brother, but perhaps it's something different." Anetolí says "Yes."[26] She makes long, thin, pendant breasts like penises, and says "This is how our breasts look when we are old."

Pattern of Hostility

Direction
1. father
3. self, mother, baby, father, mother and father

Forms
Baby: 1) throws down "by accident."
Mother: 1) (verbal) "Its anus"; 2) (verbal) "They have intercourse a great deal."
Father: 1) tries to cut head with scissors; 2) (verbal) "Its' good that way," when penis falls off; 3) (verbal) "They have intercourse a great deal."
Sister:
Elder Brother:
Self: 1) makes cutting movements on own foot with scissors.

Pattern of Sexual Objects

Direction
3. father-mother (repeatedly), baby-sister

Forms
Father-mother: 1) wants to put in position of intercourse; 2) puts penis of father doll into vagina of mother doll; 3) (verbal) "They have intercourse a great deal."
Baby-sister: 1) (verbal) "Look, Yatákana and her younger brother having intercourse. They are copulating."

Pattern of Sexual Objects

Direction
3. father-mother (twice), baby-sister, father-mother

Forms
Father-mother: 1) wants to place the father and mother in position of intercourse; 2) puts penis of father doll into vagina of mother doll; 3) (verbal) "They have intercourse a great deal."
Baby-sister: 1) (verbal) "Look, Yatákana and her younger brother are having intercourse, they are copulating."

Other Patterns

Features: treating male dolls like females. Slight overt hostility toward siblings.

[26] The kind of Pilagá "yes" that is non-committal.

YATÁKANA

Age: 5
Sex: female
Siblings: Wodyáraik, male, age 20[27]
Anetolí, female, age 9
Yalokodítn, male, age 2

Trial I. 10–13–37. Kayolí manipulates the material. Yatákana puts mother doll behind father doll. All the girls in the room begin to snap their fingers, challenging one another to box. Examiner asks Yatákana if she wants to stop. Kayolí says, "Answer her, 'Yes'." Yatákana says "Yes," and stops playing.

Trial II. 10–31–37. Removes breasts of mother doll and penis of father doll. Makes new, well-shaped breasts for the mother doll. Lapse of a few minutes while examiner treats Dañakána. After making further bids for attention Dañakána looks at examiner's blouse and says "Suña's breasts." When examiner pats her Yatákana looks daggers at Dañakána. Yatákana makes vulva for mother doll and breasts for sister doll. Picks up all the dolls but the baby doll in one hand and puts them to one side. Leaves the baby doll alone and pays no attention to it at all. Strikes Lawésakachiyi with the scissors. Lawésakachiyi dances with Naichó. Yatákana points him out to examiner and Lawésakachiyi stops, embarrassed. Yatákana puts sister and baby dolls together. Takes them away and says "They bathe." Then she stops, saying "I'll stop."

Trial III. 11–1–37. Watches other girls all the time. Picks up sister doll, says "I'll take it off," and removes breasts. Anetolí, who is present, says "Stop it!" but when examiner gives Yatákana permission, Yatákana continues. She removes breasts of mother doll. Anetolí tries to prevent her, but again permission is received from examiner and Yatákana finishes removing the breasts of the mother doll. She removes all the other parts of clay. A brief interruption while Anetolí discourses on various subjects: sorcery, the necessity for concealing food from sorcerers, Naichó the deaf and dumb girl who, Anetolí insists, is no thief. Then Yatákana makes breasts for the mother doll and the sister doll. Puts penis on father doll and puts father and mother dolls in ventral-ventral position *1*. Starts to put sister doll beside mother doll. Father doll falls off and Yatákana rights it again in ventral-ventral position with the mother. Siwóna says, "He has intercourse but he has no penis—make one." Yatákana looks at the mother doll and sees there is no genital. She says "*wu!* It has no genital." Puts penis on father doll and vulva on mother doll. The penis is small but well made. The vulva is a round blob. It looks like the breasts she has made. She takes a piece of reed from the wall of the house and presses it against the vagina, making a mark for the opening. Sister manipulates the material and Yatákana stops.

Trial IV. 11–2–37. Says: "I'll take it off," and removes breasts of sister doll. When Naichó comes to the side of the house to look in, Yatákana brandishes her arms and imitates Naichó's babbling *pyä*, *pyä*, and yells at her to go home.

[27] Married and moved out of village.

Naichó does not move. Yatákana sends father doll to look for honey, then puts it down again on the box. Picks up sister doll and says "To be sure! I'll make its breasts." Does so. She has put self and brother dolls to one side away from the others. Asks for the "widow doll." When examiner refuses it Yatákana says "I'm almost angry." When examiner asks Yatákana whether she wants to go home Yatákana says "no." When breasts of sister doll are finished she asks examiner whether that doll can be the self doll. Examiner consents and Yatákana says "I'm a beautiful little thing." Naichó is still looking in and Yatákana keeps yelling *pyä* and throwing pellets of earth at her in order to make her go away. Examiner gives Yatákana a new doll and says that this doll will now be the sister. Yatákana says, "I'll make Anetolí's breasts." She does so. Naichó is still at the door. Yatákana places father and mother in ventral-ventral position *1*, and places the penis in the vagina. She seats the baby doll beside them but with its back to them. Yatákana says, "Look at the woman, it has no breasts." Keeps motioning to Naichó to go away. Yatákana frequently has interrupted her play to run to look out of the house whenever anyone passed by. Examiner: "Do you want to stop?" Yatákana: "No." She runs back to the play box and fashions a breast. Motions to Naichó to go away. Asks to have the dolls when we go away. She has not touched the scissors although they are lying right in front of her. Takes father doll off mother doll and then removes genital of mother doll, saying "Look, this one has no breasts." Examiner tells her to make breasts, but Yatákana makes vulva. She says the mother and father dolls are having intercourse *2*. Throws earth at Naichó. Puts baby doll on father doll which she has stood up. Stands mother doll behind father doll. Puts down all the dolls. Throws a pellet at Naichó. Goes to door to strike Naichó, but Naichó runs away. Yatákana remains at the door awhile and comes back to the material. She is bored but she will not give up the dolls. Walks over to a basin of forest fruit and takes one out. Examiner suggests she eat it and Yatákana takes another. Comes back to box and picks up scissors. Cuts at the seam of her skirt and then runs to the door to strike Naichó. Comes back to the box and eats her fruit, saying "I feel like having some fruit." Puts sister doll between mother and father dolls. Wants to change name of self doll to name of examiner. Takes sister doll from its position between the mother and father dolls and puts it on the other side next to the father doll. When examiner is given a drink of water Yatákana asks for a drink. After drinking, she says "I feel like having some fruit." Asks who brought the fruit. Then she indicates the mother doll and says "Look, it has no breasts." Makes one breast and then violently pushes the father doll on the mother doll *3* while she starts another breast. Says: "I'm going to urinate, but I want to come back." Hurries back, finishes the other breast and puts it on the mother doll. Shows breasts to examiner and then says "I feel like having some fruit." Examiner tells her to take some. Yatákana takes as much as her hand will hold and comes back to the play box. She picks up all but the mother doll and says she will take them home when we leave. Tells examiner that her father will move into our house when we leave. Asks whether examiner will forbid the use of the house when she leaves the Pilagá.

Pattern of Hostility

　Direction
　　2. baby
　　4. father
　Forms
　　Baby: 1) excludes from family very pointedly.
　　Mother: 1) pushes father doll violently on mother doll.
　Restitution
　　of mother: restores breasts.
　　of sister: restores breasts.

Pattern of Sexual Objects

　Direction
　　3. father-mother
　　4. father-mother (twice)
　Forms
　　Father-mother: 1) places in ventral-ventral position; 2) (verbal) says the
　　father and mother are having intercourse; 3) pushes father doll violently
　　on mother doll.

KOITAHÁA

Age: 3 or 3½
Sex: male
Sibling: male, age 3 days

Trial I. 8–24–37. Examiner gives him the amputation doll and says "Your
father. It's a male." Koitaháa: "Its little penis. Have intercourse with her *1*. It
(the mechanical turtle) will bite me. My father, more's the pity. Its cute little
shoes." Says of a small doll: "Its arms." Says of father doll: "It is awake." Examiner: "Your younger brother is nursing." Koitaháa: "It nurses." He puts the
brother doll beside the mother doll, and says "Put a shirt on it, it is cold"

Trial II. 8–27–37. Examiner points to baby doll and says "Your younger
brother." Koitaháa: "It is weeping. It slipped" (1). Examiner tells Koitaháa to
make a penis for the father doll. Koitaháa does so and stands the doll up. Koitaháa: "Look, Jolio, it is crying hard." Examiner: "Are you weeping?" Koitaháa:
"Yes." Examiner: "Why?" Koitaháa stands up brother doll. Examiner: "You
can't. It is small." When the mother doll falls, examiner says "Your mother fell,
poor thing." Koitaháa: "It lies down." He puts self doll to the breast of mother
doll. Examiner: "Do you nurse?" Koitaháa: "It nurses." He knocks down the
mother doll (2), says "Its vagina is far in." Examiner: "Your brother is lost."
Koitaháa: "Lost. It lies down." He puts self doll next to brother doll. Says of
father doll: "It is smiling. It has a small nose." He crosses the legs of the father
doll. Examiner drops doll. Koitaháa: "It fell." He gives the doll to examiner.
Examiner: "Pity your younger brother." Koitaháa puts brother doll at breast

of mother doll. He says to himself, "*Oo oo oo.*" Plays with books for about five minutes. Examiner extends self doll to Koitaháa and says "This is you, take it." Koitaháa snatches brother doll from mother doll (3) and puts it beside self doll. Says: "Give it its companion." JH: "Take it." Koitaháa takes another doll and says "Its companion, more's the pity. It has moved its dwelling, more's the pity." He lets the mother doll fall (4). He holds the father doll upside down by the head. Tries to make it stand. Lays it down. Says of mother doll: "It's broken." He stands up a book and puts the two small dolls into it, saying "They've moved." He does the same with the mother doll, and says "It moved." He goes through the same movements with the father doll but there is no room in the book. Says of the father doll: "It moved." Examiner brings out another doll to replace the broken one. JH tells him to make breasts. Koitaháa puts them on the abdomen and puts a speck of clay on the chest. Picks up the father doll. Says: "Shall I take it (the penis) off?" JH: "No." Koitaháa: "Look at its anus." Removes the penis (5). Koitaháa: "Look, it came off." Examiner: "Give me your younger brother." Koitaháa throws over the doll. Examiner: "Give me Koitaháa." Koitaháa: "It is not here." He will not give up the doll. Examiner: "Give it to me." Koitaháa: "It is not here." At last he takes it out and reluctantly holds it up. Examiner: "Does it want to nurse?" Koitaháa: "Yes. I want to take it to my mother." Examiner: "The mother's breast came off." Koitaháa replaces the breast. Examiner turns over the toy box and it rattles. Koitaháa: "Jolio, were you afraid?" JH: "Yes. Were you?" Koitaháa: "Yes." Examiner: "Your father." Koitaháa: "He is working. I burn it" (6).

Examiner leaves with Koitaháa after giving him a baby doll. When examiner and Koitaháa arrive at Koitaháa's house his mother is sitting outside, her baby on the ground beside her, her dress rolled up exposing her breasts. Koitahá pulls down the dress, covering her breasts. Then he lifts the dress again and puts the face of his doll against her breast, saying "It is nursing."

Pattern of Hostility

  Direction
  1. father
  2. brother, mother, brother, mother, father

  Forms
  Baby: 1) (verbal) "It is weeping. It slipped"; 2) removes from breast.
  Mother: 1) knocks down; 2) lets fall.
  Father: 1) (verbal) "My father, more's the pity"; 2) removes penis; 3) (verbal) "I burn it."
  Self:

Pattern of Sexual Objects

  Direction
  1. father-uncertain

  Forms
  Father-uncertain: "Have intercourse with her."

SIWÓNA

Age: 7–8
Sex: female

Siblings: This child had three siblings by two different fathers. Her own father was dead and she was his only child. Siwóna was only a visitor in our village and we did not know her siblings. In her experiment, however, she manipulated only one child doll of the four.

Trial I. 11–2–37. Puts a child doll into her mouth. The head and half of the body are in her mouth. Asks for the new mother doll. Examiner says it is a widow and can not emerge from retirement. Siwóna takes it seriously and says, "When she has been a long time a widow she will emerge from her concealment." Points to father doll and says "That is her second husband." Puts the child doll into the arms of the father doll and says "Going to defecate, more's the pity." Walks the doll back. Brings it to the toy box and says, "Bringing her grandchild, but its grandmother is a widow." Puts father doll and children dolls back on the play box. Puts the same child doll she has been playing with inside her own blouse on her breast. Takes it out and says "My daughter." The children outside are trying to come in again. Examiner asks Siwóna if she wants to stop. She says "Yes" unwillingly, and goes out.

NAKÍNAK, KUWASIÑÍTN, WETÉL, YORODAIKOLÍK

In this trial the dolls represent Nakínak's family but they are manipulated by the four boys. The dolls are: mother, father, brother, self, baby sister.

JH puts baby doll to nurse. Wetél says "Oma'í's[28] penis" (1). Nakínak just sits there and does nothing. Now he puts brother doll on mother doll *1*. Wetél puts brother doll on mother doll *2*. Nakínak takes it off, scowling. Wetél puts brother doll on Nakínak doll *3*, then on father doll *4*. Kuwasiñítn says "Tiny anus" (2). He puts brother doll on father doll, penises touching *5*. Yorodaikolík puts Nakínak doll on brother doll *6*. It falls. Wetél very carefully puts penis of Nakínak doll into anus of brother doll *7*. Yorodaikolík says "They are having intercourse in the anus" (3) *8*. Nakínak pinches him. Wetél puts baby doll face down on mother doll *9* in position of intercourse. Kuwasiñítn puts penis of brother doll in his own mouth *10*. He puts father doll on mother doll in position of intercourse *11*. Nakínak removes the father doll. Wetél puts brother doll on mother doll, saying "He has intercourse" *12*. He puts penis of brother doll into anus of Nakínak doll *13*. He says, "He has intercourse in the anus" (4). Kuwasiñítn complains that the penis of the father doll came off. Nakínak takes brother doll off self doll. Wetél growls and says "He is having intercourse." He replaces the dolls *14*. Kuwasiñítn puts Nakínak doll on father doll *15*. Wetél puts Nakínak doll on mother doll *16*. He tries to spread legs of mother doll but cannot. He puts Nakínak doll on mother doll, the penis in the vagina *17*. Kuwasiñítn puts a huge vulva on baby doll and

---

[28] Nakínak's father.

puts breasts on the father doll. Puts father doll on mother doll *18*, saying: "Oma'í is having intercourse" (*5*). Wetél says "He has intercourse" (6), and puts brother doll on Nakínak doll *19*. He names the dolls as he does this, calling them Adíechi[29] and Nakínak. Kuwasiñítn puts father doll on mother doll *20* and brother doll on top of father doll *21*. "Nakínak has intercourse with his sister" (7) says Wetél putting Nakínak doll on baby doll *22*. They leave the dolls in position of intercourse and just sit looking at them. Wetél says "I'll have intercourse with you." Kuwasiñítn says "Look, Wetél's back is roasted."[30] Kuwasiñítn puts father doll next to brother doll, but then changes it, laying the Nakínak doll next to the father doll. Kuwasiñítn lays father doll on mother doll *23*, saying "Intercourse." Then he says, "He has his head in his hands." The penis of the Nakínak doll falls off and Kuwasiñítn puts one on. Nakínak sets up father doll. Yorodaikolík puts it down on all fours. Nakínak puts it on its feet. Kuwasiñítn takes it way. Nakínak sets up brother doll but Wetél snatches it. Wetél says of baby doll, "Where are its feet? Where is its vulva? Jolio, it has no vulva." After a few minutes of inaction, Yorodaikolík says "I am going." Kuwasiñítn says "Go, he chased you." Nakínak sets up father doll. He names the brother doll, saying "Adíechi." When Kuwasiñítn says that Nakínak's mother and father are having intercourse Nakínak does not respond. "Adíechi's mother," (8) says Kuwasiñítn, putting brother doll and mother doll in position of intercourse *24*. Kuwasiñítn removes brother doll. Nakínak takes it but puts it aside. He tries to put the brother doll on top of the mother and father dolls *25*. Kuwasiñítn takes it away. Nakínak puts the brother doll back on top of the copulating mother and father dolls *26* and says "Nóroi."[31] When Kuwasiñítn puts the brother doll on top of the mother and father dolls *27*, Nakínak shakes the box. Nakínak puts the self doll next to the baby doll which is next to the mother doll. He tries hard. He tries to put a penis on the self doll. Kuwasiñítn takes away the doll to make a penis. Nakínak sets up the father doll and fixes the penis.

Of the total of 35 moves and remarks directed specifically toward sexual objects, 17 refer to homosexual objects, 15 to heterosexual objects, and 3 are uncertain.

[29] Adíechi is Nakínak's step-brother.
[30] Wetél's back was once burnt.
[31] An old female neighbor of the boys.

BIBLIOGRAPHY

1. BATESON, G. *Culture Contact and Schismogenesis.* Man, December, 1935.
2. HENRY, J. *Some Cultural Determinants of Hostility in Pilagá Indian Children.* Am. J. Orthopsychiatry, X: 1, 1940.
3. ——— *A Method for Learning to Talk Primitive Languages.* Am. Anthropologist, 42: 4, 1940.
4. ——— *The Linguistic Position of the Ashluslay.* Intern. J. Am. Linguistics, X: 2–3, 1939.
5. ——— *Jungle People.* J. J. Augustin, New York. 1941.
6. ——— and ZUNIA. *Speech Disturbances in Pilagá Indian Children.* Am. J. Orthopsychiatry, X: 2, 1940.
7. HENRY, JULES and ZUNIA, and ANNA HARTOCH SCHACHTEL. *Rorschach Analysis of Pilagá Indian Children.* Ibid., XII: 4, 1942.
8. ——— JULES and ZUNIA. *Symmetrical and Reciprocal Hostility in Sibling Rivalry.* Ibid., 2, 1942.
9. KLEIN, MELANIE. *The Psychoanalysis of Children.* Hogarth Press, London, 1932.
10. LEVY, DAVID M. *Sibling Rivalry.* Research Monographs No. 2. Am. Orthopsychiatric Assoc. 1937.
11. ——— *Sibling Rivalry Studies in Children of Primitive Groups.* Am. J. Orthopsychiatry, IX: 1, 1939.
12. MEAD, MARGARET. *Cooperation and Competition among Primitive Peoples.* McGraw-Hill Book Co., New York, 1937.
13. ——— *More Comprehensive Field Methods.* Am. Anthropologist, 35: 1, 1933.
14. MURPHY, GARDNER, LOIS BARCLAY MURPHY, and THEODORE NEWCOMB. *Experimental Social Psychology.* Harper and Bro., New York, 1937.

JULES HENRY was born in New York City in 1904. He studied under Franz Boas and Ruth Benedict at Columbia University, where he received his doctorate in anthropology in 1936. Dr. Henry taught at Columbia University, the University of Chicago, and until his death in 1969, at Washington University in St. Louis.

He was a Research Associate at the Sonia Shankman Orthogenic School and was a Fellow at the Center for Advanced Study in the Behavioral Sciences at Stanford. He also served as consultant to the National Institute of Mental Health and the World Health Organization, among others, as well as a number of psychiatric hospitals. His articles have been widely published in professional and general journals. He is the author of *Jungle People, Culture Against Man, Pathways to Madness, On Education*, and *On Sham, Vulnerability and Other Forms of Self-Destruction*.

ZUNIA HENRY lives in St. Louis.